IT'S ON YOU

Empowerment for Leaders Seeking the Highest Level of Personal Satisfaction and Corporate Success

MARTHA BROWN
with Joscelyn Duffy

REDWOOD PUBLISHING, LLC

Published by:
Redwood Publishing, LLC
www.redwooddigitalpublishing.com
Orange County, California

ISBN: 979-8-9906149-0-1 (hardcover)
ISBN: 979-8-9906149-1-8 (paperback)
ISBN: 979-8-9906149-3-2 (e-book)

Library of Congress Control Number: 2024914213

Interior Design:
Jose Pepito

Cover Design:
Michelle Manley

Cover Photo:
Author photo by Brent Cline

Expanded Praise for *It's On You*

"I enjoyed reading Martha Brown's book *It's On You* because it wasn't fancy; rather it was honest. We live in a time of great advancements like Artificial Intelligence and business heroes like Elon Musk. But the reality is business competence and team engagement are at all time lows. Martha 're-introduces' us to the powerful concepts of self improvement, showing up for your team, staying open to new ideas ... and just trying hard. She does so using industries and references we can all understand. If you are like me ... and sick of reading tweets and business buzzwords ... pick up *It's On You*. It will make you want to try harder!"

—Jeff Immelt, Retired CEO, GE;
venture partner; Founder, JACS Capital

"It's On You is your light at the end of the tunnel. If you are questioning what's next for you as a leader, this deeply practical guide will lead you to identify your potential and pinpoint how to focus your efforts, so you can reach that higher gear of ultimate fulfillment and success."

—Frances Frei, Professor, Harvard Business School

"Martha Brown makes sense of the everyday challenges and dilemma facing any entrepreneur. Her down-to-earth approach gives the business leader permission to reexamine their everyday team management, via their own self-understanding. Under Martha's thoughtful guidance, the potential leader will understand the need and responsibility to hone their own instincts before they can improve their company's everyday efficacity. She gives permission to be less busy, to be more creative, more compassionate. To accept and embrace a role as a true, brave, caring and reliable leader in this crazy world. Step into your power, because success really is on you."

—Sharon Santoni, Author, Publisher, Entrepreneur & CEO, My French Country Home

"Martha Brown puts you in the driver's seat and gives you a one-way ticket to the next level of self-realization and success you have long held in your heart. ... Whether you are new to leadership or a veteran of the corner office, her practical and personal prescription will give you what it takes to relentlessly show up, step up, and soar into your authentic potential."

—Kurt Graves, Executive Coach and Vistage Chair of CEO Peer Groups

"It's time to become the leader you have always wanted to be. In *It's On You*, veteran CEO, Martha Brown offers a clear and candid approach to the deeply human aspects of leadership. Her unique insights take you to a place where thinking about how you are showing up can directly and positively impact the pragmatic aspects of your day-to-day satisfaction and success."

—E. Elisabet Lahti, Ph.D., Founder, Sisu Lab & Author, *Gentle Power*

CONTENTS

CURIOSITY AND CREATIVITY

LEADING WITH CARE

DOGGED DETERMINATION

III. SHAPING A ROADMAP FOR CONTINUED SUCCESS

FOREWORD

by E. Elisabet Lahti, Ph.D.
CEO, Sisu Lab & Author, *Gentle Power*

IN LEADERSHIP, POWER is fundamental—it is expressed in every conversation, relationship, and decision. Executives, endurance athletes, entrepreneurs, and adventurers are all often applauded for the willpower, dogged mental endurance, and resilience that empower them to navigate great challenges and excel amid even the most unimaginable circumstances. All too often, however, such power and strength are equated with force and domination, while concepts like stillness, introspection, listening, and compassion are dubbed "soft" or "weak." But it is these "softer" aspects—those founded in awareness and love—that are key to helping you realize the totality of the personal satisfaction or corporate success that awaits you.

During the pursuit of my doctoral dissertation to study the lived experience of what in my native Finland is called *sisu*—extraordinary perseverance and fortitude in the face of extreme adversity—I ran and cycled 1,500 miles across the length of New Zealand in fifty days, using a phenomenological and auto-ethnographical research framework. As the days stretched on, extraordinary perseverance became critical in allowing me to access my second, third, and fourth winds throughout the ultrarunning. I wandered into the various unknown edges of my mental, physical, and existential landscapes, and I became acutely aware of the unexplored edges of my potential, which stretched further than I could ever have assumed simply by imagining them. At various points, a newfound fire within emerged, driving me beyond these previously perceived boundaries and pushing me forward into the unknown with a new sense of confidence and capacity.

As a leader, you spend your days running the ultramarathon of navigating the countless facets of guiding others and directing business. You do so as signals of instant danger are sprung upon you and challenges loom large, yet you too choose to continuously charge toward the unknown and stretch the boundaries of what you believe to be possible. You do so because a leader is who you are at heart, and you want to continue enriching the totality of who and what you are in order to better ride the waves of challenge and serve others in the greatest capacity possible—one that helps you, your team, and your company to realize your ultimate potential.

In today's uncertain, continuously evolving, ever-changing world, there exists a glaring need for a new direction and form of leadership. Times like the pandemic have pushed us all to the brink of previous capacities, as organizations and institutions have been tested like never before. This has left you and all leaders at a crossroads of choice—a decision point that can elicit and bring to the forefront a new power previously unawakened within yourself, within your team, and within your company as a whole.

As mentioned before, the Finnish concept of *sisu* represents the hidden strength found after the furthest edge of our assumed capacity and strength has been reached; it is that next breath, step, and heartbeat, or the seemingly impossible action or decision taken when the scale could tip either way or is in fact in favor of tipping backward. I have defined *sisu* as "a universal quality of extraordinary perseverance, action-mindset, and latent power in the face of extreme adversity." In its higher expression, *sisu* is what I call "gentle power"—a quality that can be cultivated and which offers a harmonious and helpful approach to making decisions, relating to one another, and viewing ourselves in times of both rocky waters and smoother seas. This graceful expression of the embodied fortitude of *sisu* breaches the boundaries of stamina or resolve, allowing us to go unyieldingly beyond previous perceived or imagined limits ... though we must always remain cognizant of the need to use this power wisely, as fire can either burn down the house or be used to cook a meal. That is why the responsibility, as Ms. Brown's book title not only suggests but I believe implores, "is on you."

Our deepest strengths and greatest success have everything to do with both ownership of our power and gentleness toward ourselves and others. Approaching your leadership from an internal orientation opens the portal to not only strong and powerful action, but also long-sighted and uplifting direction for those you serve. While the gentle power of *sisu* can be a guiding force for anyone in a CEO or leadership role, its true strength lies in exercising proactivity and response rooted in awareness. It is about how well you prepare yourself for the unexpected. It is, perhaps most important, about your awareness of yourself and others. *Sisu,* much like Martha Brown's work, is less about success or achievement for achievement's sake and more about giving the situation—be it a self-chosen challenge or an unexpected hardship hurled upon us—our all, and then some. That "then some" portion is firmly rooted in the higher-octave expression of *sisu*—that which is not blind and obsessive but adaptive, conscious, reasonable, and harmonious.

Leadership must always be approached with what Esa Saarinen, Rachel Jones, and Raimo P. Hämäläinen describe in their 2014 book *Being Better Better: Living with Systems Intelligence* as a "higher-level orientation." This involves stretching and challenging yourself to improve on a daily basis in order to overcome limiting conditionings and unleash the totality of your true, remarkable inner fortitude. Research supports the idea that practices related to personal reflection, emotional regulation, self-compassion, and mindfulness (i.e., awareness of inner states, including cognitive and somatic phenomena), as well as mental preparation through priming or visualizing the event beforehand, are beneficial in creating the optimal performance state. It simply requires deliberate practice, along with great awareness, strength, resilience, and mentorship from others who have walked the path before you.

In *It's On You*, veteran CEO Martha Brown takes a clear and candid approach to the real human aspects of leadership and how your willingness to think about what you are thinking (and doing) can directly and positively impact the pragmatic aspects of your day-to-day satisfaction and success. She offers practical strategies and thought-provoking exercises strategically designed to build the internal fortitude you need to take on tomorrow and reach for that next-next level, and to do so in a way that is true to the leader you want to be.

Whether you are aiming to lead an organization someday or find yourself seated in the CEO seat today, stepping into the role of executive leadership will be a beautiful (and at times extremely challenging) dance of gentle power and your ability to awaken to your full capacity. If you wish to take yourself and your organization to points far beyond previously, and allow a determination fueled by awareness and gentle assuredness to propel you forward, I urge you to embrace and take to heart what Martha Brown clearly and beautifully portrays. Because the greatest power in leadership is a gentle one; it is a power best discovered when you go where the silence is and listen deeply within yourself and to what your team members have been saying. I invite you to immerse yourself in this adventure and share in Martha's practical and insightful teachings that will help you hone your leadership niche and find great personal satisfaction and success. As you do, may you grow your "gentle power," as it invites you to discern not just *what* you do, but also *how* you do what you do ... thereby allowing you to go more knowingly and confidently into the unknown of your fullest and highest expression.

—E. Elisabet Lahti, PhD; CEO, Sisu Lab; Author, *Gentle Power*

If you realized that all the success you desire lies within you, would you take the journey there?

A JOURNEY TO CEO

Courage creates a flywheel
effect in our lives.

"I THINK YOU need to be our next CEO," said my brother, Byron.

"Really?" I asked.

"Yeah," Byron said.

And that was that. I would be CEO.

It was July 2012, and our company's owners were gathered around the conference room table holding our annual board meeting with Byron at the helm as our current CEO. We were discussing next steps and what succession would look like after Byron retired.

I was just sitting there doing my thing, quietly taking the minutes, when from seemingly out of nowhere, Byron made his suggestion. I remember looking up at my brother-in-law, Mike across the room and seeing him literally jump in his seat. Nobody was ready for it, including me. The opportunity to step into the role of CEO filled me with equal parts surprise, utter shock, and delight. Byron's announcement came at a time in my life when I was emerging from a great transition and some deeply introspective work. Yet I knew my brother had clear reasons for doing everything he did, which was often informed equally by his intellect and his gut.

My head started running quickly through countless plans for my leadership. I would write them out on index cards and Post-it notes and watch them quickly turn into a quest shaped around one prominent question: *How will I bring value to my company today?* Though I had been nurturing my own confidence, I knew the role of CEO would bring entirely new challenges. I would be tasked with leading and empowering the team I had been part of for many years. I had always seen their potential and known that they were hungry, I hadn't previously been in a position to do more than encourage them when and where I could. I also felt that up till then, I hadn't had the credibility to help elevate them. Now, as CEO, I would. I could step up and lead my team—and it was daunting because the voices of my inner perfectionist and my fear had joined the party, whispering not-so-sweet nothings in my ear. Could I really do this?

My parents founded our multi-generational, privately held home furnishing and interior design company, Tipperary Sales, in 1976, and immediately gave it to their children. Byron and Mike ran the company together, with my sister, Charlotte, choosing to stay home and raise her family, which was arguably the more challenging role. In 1989, I joined the company after graduating from college, and spent the bulk of my years in operations—accounting, inventory control, sales management, and then marketing. Outside of whatever my title was, or my role dictated, I also completed any special tasks Byron asked of me. The learning never stopped. I had my human moments, where I questioned my future and whether I really wanted to stay with the company. But as I continued to put myself in positions where I could keep growing by facing challenges and pushing my own boundaries, all roads increasingly led back to remaining in the family business.

"You've done everything at this company," Byron reminded me. He felt that my becoming CEO was the next logical progression, and his belief in me strengthened my belief in myself. Byron and Charlotte have always been like Mars and Venus influences in my life. Both are role models to me, for very different reasons. My sister taught me gentleness, kindness, and compassion. Byron taught me how to think tactically, fight strategically, and develop mental toughness. They have loved me unconditionally, especially at times when I needed it most. Charlotte has been my ever-present cheerleader, and Byron, my mirror. Their love and faith in me absolutely fueled my drive to fulfill the role of CEO in the best and largest way possible.

In the days that followed the meeting that changed my life, Byron continued to support me, challenging me to elevate my own potential and suggesting that I look into business classes to brush up on my business acumen before accepting the CEO reins. It would have been much easier to haphazardly take a few business courses that may or may not have filled in gaps of my knowledge, or to have hired a coach or mentor, but in typical Martha fashion I sought to keep pushing to see just how far I could grow. I applied for the Executive MBA program at the McColl School of Business at Queens University of Charlotte, North Carolina—a program built on former Bank of America CEO and Chairman Hugh McColl's three C's of Leadership: Competence, Character, and Commitment to Community[1]—and just to make things really interesting, I moved to an entirely new city and state to attend the program and start this new chapter.

Going back to school to learn from professors who either owned businesses or were working for large multi-national corporations was one of the most terrifying, challenging, and fulfilling things I've ever done. At forty-five, I was the second-oldest person in the class, and I was truly worried my brain wouldn't work as it had twenty-five years prior, when I was getting my undergraduate degree. When I got accepted into the program, my first thought was that I was the admission team's mistake—at least until the dean addressed the entire MBA class on the first day, saying, "I know each of you are sitting there wondering if you are the admission's mistake." In that moment, I realized I wasn't alone. As terrified as I was of failing, I felt sure, from that moment on, that I was on the right track.

When I started these studies, I had just moved from being chief communications officer into the role of president, all while establishing myself in a new community. The cumulative demands were adding up and the Executive MBA program proved intense. When I signed up, I thought I'd walk out of the two-year program with revolutionary ideas about how to change our operations or accounting systems. To everyone's surprise, 70% of the curriculum was centered on leadership teachings, real organizational behavior (i.e., understanding the impact of how you show up as a leader), and how to become a self-actualized leader and what that meant.

An unwavering need to be, do, and have it all drove me through the first year of juggling the program with my work commitments; though by the start of the second year of the MBA, I felt I had run out of gas. I was having those dangerous but necessary conversations with myself about whether to let myself off the hook and only complete the first year. But since I had always been unwilling to abandon a big mission, I found it within myself to push forward, driven by a fierce sense of loyalty and dedication to the opportunities that had been given to me. Receiving my diploma from university president Pamela Davies reminded me of what I could truly do, even in those moments of second-guessing myself. In my final review, the head of the MBA program, Bill Berry, said that I "came in with the least to gain and left with the most."

Three months after I graduated, I took the reins as CEO. I took on new reports and enveloped myself in the role driven by a deep desire to understand every one of the people and processes involved. I built a forward-facing platform, working toward my vision for the company. There were opportunities to create new work and new positions, and I tasked myself with personally assigning job responsibilities, salaries, and operational structures. There were promotions that needed to happen, so I looked at the organizational chart and strategically plotted. With so much to be done, my first year found me overworking, overthinking, and utterly exhausted. While working to scratch, scrape, and deal with the pressure of the new role, I had my fair share of *oh crap!* moments, but when things were going right, it felt like riding a bike for the first time: *I'm doing it! I'm doing it! Look at me, I'm doing it!*

For some, riding a bike may sound like an easy feat, but I learned to ride a bike on a dirt road in the Sandhills of South Carolina—terrain hardly ideal for maneuvering a Raleigh 3-speed. Skidding out was guaranteed, and the sand was sure to create great sinkholes for my wheels to disappear into. It was often a struggle to get traction, and in those first few years as CEO, I frequently had the feeling of trying to get traction in those sand hills all over again. I sometimes felt I was spinning my wheels, trying to find my way back to my own confidence, but in retrospect I think that was just my humility. People would tell me they loved how I taught, that they thought my vision and ideas were great, and that things weren't falling apart, but I still didn't always feel that I was crushing the CEO gig. Things "not falling apart" was not what I was shooting for. I wanted so badly to see the team and organization truly thrive, but I was missing the point. I wasn't allowing myself to believe in myself, my journey, my education, the feedback I was getting from key people in my life, or what I felt my contribution was to the role of CEO. When I allowed myself to make silence one of my greatest allies, to gain greater self-awareness, and to operate more confidently from my authenticity, things became smoother and easier.

I learned from my MBA that the most important thing any of us can work on is our own leadership, so that's what I did. Five years into my new role, I found my groove, and things kept building from there. There would always be room to grow and change for the better. There would be failures en route and I would try things that didn't work, but I believed that eventually the odds would work out in my favor, and they did. During my time as CEO, we grew an award-winning team of 170 employees and realized a compound annual growth rate (CAGR) of 17% in revenue and eclipsed more than $70 million in sales. *Furniture Today*, the industry's premier publication, named our company one of the top 100 furniture stores in America multiple years over. Several of our stores were ranked in the top 10 in North America, and we were repeatedly home to the top designer in the Southeast. The success felt great, but I was also acutely aware of how I had to get through the tough, heavy-duty learning times and tractionless hills to get there.

Courage creates a flywheel effect in our lives. My personal courage workout of stepping into the unknown territory of new leadership roles in our organization ended up paying off, propelling me into significant areas of opportunity and achievement. In the grander scheme of things, becoming CEO began to feel like my destiny, my calling. It was one of the greatest personal growth journeys I could have asked for, and most definitely what God intended me to do. I brought all of myself to the table, and the "Martha package" became a beautiful synergy of those indisputable moments pursuing that something more, all bundled up with those moments of all-too-human self-doubt, grit, and faith to overcome the fear.

Sometimes we don't know what we want to do, have, or be until someone or something opens the door to us doing it. Personally, I don't think I ever truly imagined that I would be able to be CEO, because I didn't know I wanted it until Byron "asked" me to do it. Even so, I could not and would not have accepted the role without a deep internal desire and drive to do it, and to do it well. I knew I would be pushed to help my team and company grow, but the day I stepped into the role, there really was no predicting just how much the opportunity would help me grow as a human being and a leader. Today, my greatest satisfaction is being able to teach others the how-to of being a CEO and help them find their groove, their voice, and what they uniquely bring to the table. This may be my story, but it can also be yours. When you say a big YES to the opportunities to rise into a leadership or CEO role, you are saying yes to opening up your personal growth in an incredible way—that is, if you are willing to step into the silence and embrace the journey of looking inside yourself.

No matter how great your achievements to date, they will pale in comparison to your potential and the opportunity that lies in wait, when you learn to tap that potential. You already have inside of you all that you need to fulfill what is possible for yourself and your organization. The only question now is: *Are you ready?*

THIS IS YOUR LAUNCH POINT

*If you don't know where you are
going, any path will get you there.*

WHAT IS GOING right in your leadership? What is not,
and why? Where is it that you want to be—as a human
being, as a leader, as an organization? What needs to
happen to get you "there"—stretching you to points C,
D, E, and beyond?

Chances are, from one perspective or another, you
have questioned the bigger picture of your ultimate potential. You are a natural leader who has worked hard
to get where you are, and you are not afraid to do what
it takes to get from A to B. You are here because you
want to get "there"—to that next level of success and

fulfillment. Yet despite your ambition, proactivity, and growth orientation, the path forward doesn't always seem clear or feel easy. At times, a fear of failure holds you back from fully accepting or reaching for that leadership role you've always dreamed of. You struggle (perhaps sometimes secretly) with self-doubt, worry that you are going to somehow mishandle or mislead your team, or think that people won't take you seriously. The truth is that beyond the dogged determination and achievement orientation that most recognize you for, you are also very human!

Change is the only constant, and because change never stops, growth opportunities never stop. When you are willing to question what is going right (and not right) with your current leadership, the next question should always be, *What do I want to do now?* What are you doing today to become a better CEO and organization? Though change is inescapable, *you* get to inform the script. That said, not every step has to be monumental, nor every decision earth-shattering. Sometimes it's the smallest moments of silent awareness that have the biggest impact on your leadership and on those who feel the ensuing ripple effects. Give yourself the opportunity to "not know," and to question who you want to be and where you want to go. Then you get to choose how and when you progress forward. You have the ability to make a positive impact with every step you take, and it all begins with the launch point of identifying who you are and what you want—what success looks like for you—and dedicating yourself wholeheartedly to that.

In my journey up the ladder into greater leadership roles and eventually to CEO, I could never seem to find exactly the right book to inform me of the myriad ways I felt influenced or could influence as a leader—one that addressed all of the elements of what it meant to be human and navigating the constant twists, turns, and questioning of my leadership potential. Without factoring in the unexpected bumps and the human elements that remain very real in every day of business, any clear-cut direction can quickly turn into a one-way ticket to nowhere. It was only when I went into the silence of my own thoughts and self that I discovered the puzzle pieces I sought . . . and as many greats have said, once you learn, teach. And so, I decided to write the guidebook I always dreamed of having, in hopes that it may be what you have been seeking to help you engage daily to become a better CEO, leading a better organization.

There is no greater gift you can give to those you lead than to be a positive example, and no more noble cause than to help others see their own worth and be encouraged along their own journey. Those who are served well by your leadership will go on to have their own voice and bring their own unique gifts and talents to the table. This form of leadership builds a positive-momentum cycle for the company. Other CEOs will talk about legacy, and while I like the word and the spirit of it, this work is not about posting our names on the front of a building occupied by a company we have built. More so, this work is about answering this question:

What did I do to create goodness that others can take and build upon in ways that will also be good?

Success can and will mean change within your organization. It can mean leaving or changing a role, and change of any kind is hard. Some days you're going to take one step forward and fall three steps back. But the common denominator to every evolving success story is that a great personal-growth journey begins with a strategic launch point. When there is somewhere you want to be, you need to ask yourself what you want to do about it. What is your launch point? What is your next step? That is where you begin, and this book has been designed for the aspiring leader or CEO to find your way from "here" to "there." *It's On You* is designed for those who are inclined toward leadership or those of you who have been thrust into a CEO role and are trying to find your way. This book does not contain a simple 7-step plan to magically conjure success, nor is it an operational manual on how to run your company or department. It is a guide for those who are fueled by a curiosity about opening up their next level of leadership, fulfillment, and success, and for those who have a fervent desire for personal and professional growth. In the following pages, you will find proven strategies that will allow you to fulfill the real need to get things done in your day-to-day leadership as you continue to grow into who you can become … all the while realizing the personal satisfaction of it all.

There is no straight line or smooth path to success as a leader. You can experience growth and realize new levels of positive impact, potential, and personal satisfaction, and help create the same for others—yet such an awakening must come in tandem with effectively managing the current day-to-day challenges of being a leader. This is not a free-for-all, nor is it permission to flip everything on its head. You still have to be producing and moving forward on a daily basis, using the tools you have tested over time and know will work. This work honors the real journey you are facing, internally and externally, every single day, because what matters is not how the road to success looks, but how you handle it. Your leadership potential isn't solely about knowing your worth and living true to it when times are good; it's equally about what you do when times are tough. The fulfillment of your potential requires a stair-step journey of building self-awareness. It is a process that evolves when you realize what you need to work on every step of the way. Even if you have bumps and bruises, you get right back on the metaphorical bike and keep pedaling ahead. And as you do, you must be willing to continuously go within yourself and do the harder work to achieve the bigger, longer-lasting, more rewarding results.

This work can plant seeds. If you internalize the principles and do the work, you can flourish the way you want and shape the team you deserve. From today forward, may you give yourself permission to not know all the answers and have the courage to say there is more that you are capable of becoming. The *It's On You* journey of coaching yourself toward authentic success and satisfaction flows through three phases, all driven by the vision of going within to be the best leader you can be:

1. **Showing Up**

   Everything, including the ability to identify your personal and professional potential, begins with your willingness to show up authentically. This includes awareness of yourself, your differences, your "State of Being," and how you are being received. (More on "State of Being" on page 62.)

2. Stepping into Your Potential

Realizing your potential requires a foundation of behaviors that will lead to your desired results. This step involves doing the required work to define the unique behaviors that will help you step into your power.

3. Shaping a Road Map for Continued Success

Progress in the face of unexpected challenges and indirect paths requires clear metrics and a steadfast dedication. When you learn to navigate the not-so-smooth roads with grace, you move yourself and your organization ever closer to the realization of your ultimate potential.

No one can tell you how to run your company or department. Just the same, no one can tell you exactly how to progress to realize your ultimate leadership potential and success. The best thing anyone can do for you is provide the principles and strategies to guide you. The *It's On You* principles are time-tested and designed to help you find the path to your ultimate success—one that includes personal satisfaction and fulfillment. They are nuggets of encouragement and insights aimed at the vulnerability you may feel about not yet having the confidence to be the leader you want to be. They only require that you adapt them to your circumstances, because this is not a one-size-fits-all solution. The principles here have been designed to speak to the universality of being human, which means adopting them while remaining open to making any required adjustments to the length or direction of your specific success journey and the needs of the people and organization you serve.

You have what it takes to lead at the highest level, and every day you can choose to coach yourself up rather than coach yourself out. You can elevate the questions you are asking and the results you are realizing. The *It's On You* method is a process of lifelong learning, designed to help you find your niche, define your path, and discover all the personal satisfaction that goes along with that. It will help you become the leader who helps others discover *their* potential. Let yourself be who you authentically are, and let this book be your guide on the journey of leadership—keeping in mind that sometimes, all you need to do is get out of your own way.

I.

SHOWING UP

Everything starts with how you show up. The
leader you become begins with your willingness
to have self-awareness, to be different, and
to learn from the journey as you go.

WE GET THE TEAMS WE DESERVE

What happens in the company, whether
victory or failure, is on you.

ARE YOUR NUMBERS not where you want them to be? Do you see factions or silos forming across the organization? Are there failures in communication within your team? Have the recent company survey scores come back looking not so great? Or are you too afraid to do a survey because you don't want to know what others think?

As a CEO or leader, you are a center point in your organization. As the leader goes, the company goes.

Everything that happens in the company or within your team, whether victory or failure, *is ultimately on you*. If your team is dysfunctional or your team is not a team, that's on you. Everything that exists within your organization at this very moment *starts with you*. While this statement may sound harsh, it is actually a source of great empowerment, directing your awareness to the impact your everyday behaviors and actions can have on the whole. The good news here is that the heights of success and the realization of your true personal and organizational potential are also on you, and you get to write the script for this story.

When I read former Navy SEALs Jocko Willink and Leif Babin's 2015 #1 *New York Times* bestseller *Extreme Ownership*, one particular aspect of their message really hit home. Jocko stated that the leader must own every failure, but the team owns every victory. In his TEDx Talk by the same name as his book, he tells the story of submitting a report up the chain of command as to why his wartime team had opened fire on their own and taken the life of an Iraqi soldier. When it came time for the debriefing, Jocko had one simple question for everyone in a room that included his injured colleague:

"Whose fault was this?" One after the other, the SEALs raised their hands and gave their reasons for why they were taking ownership for what had happened. After listening to each of them, Jocko claimed ultimate responsibility. He was the leader, and he believed that the failure of the mission was on him. He said it hurt his ego and his pride to take the blame, but to maintain his integrity as a leader he had to take responsibility.[2] In the end, his choice not to pass on the burden of blame led to greater respect from his men and commanding officer.

This was a tough concept for me to accept at first—not so much the part about claiming responsibility but the one about not being able to claim wins as a leader. As CEO, I know how hard I work for our victories to rectify our misses, and naturally I would like to be able to celebrate the wins. Both aspects of this failures-and-victories concept force us to really examine our egos so that we can give our teams the kudos for the win. Then we must give ourselves the focus to unpack the failures and shepherd them into the next wins, which will once again go to the team.

Over the years, my business coach and the chair of our Vistage CEO group, Kurt Graves, has gifted me with many insights and helped me see this "energy piece." When you are CEO or a leader, the people who make up your company or team are going to take on your energy, your voice, your mission, and your core values. A company is a living, breathing, organic being, because it is made up of people. Kurt has helped me walk back to the junctions where I've made assumptions, and he has talked me off some cliffs while pushing me to leap off others. And he told me something I will never forget: "We get the teams we deserve." This is to say that there is an undeniable link between the status of one's team and a leader or CEOs who doesn't want to claim responsibility to own the challenges and chaos within their organization. For those trained and raised in business, there is a propensity to think that the CEO has all the answers and can never be brought to task (except by the board of directors when you are not making your numbers). That kind of thinking is playing small, and I'm here to relieve you of that burden. It's time to play big and step into the scene of human capacity and potential. If things are off or there exists great pain or challenge within your company, it's time for you to take ownership and help turn things around.

"It's on you" is not a statement of blame or shame; it is one of ownership and accountability. It's about being an active participant in all aspects of what could be better within your organization. The hard truth is that if you are a CEO or leader, you accepted this responsibility when you said yes to your role. Fixing the challenges that exist within your organization may be interpreted as a heavy burden, though it's important to understand that endeavoring to do so can also present a life-changing and deeply impactful opportunity.

As the leader of (or in) your business, *you* ultimately get to decide who joins your company, and you can create the hiring protocol to find them. But even before that, you get to decide what you want your culture to look like, feel like, and work like. *You* have the opportunity to build teams that are stoked and satisfied. *You* have the opportunity to empower your team members to do their jobs brilliantly and operate with higher levels of performance and personal satisfaction. But it all revolves around how you show up for your team, each and every day.

Understanding how everything that happens in the company or within your team, whether victory or failure, *is on you*, is the first piece of the puzzle—a launch point that opens the door to your being all you can be as a leader. When you make the connection between who you are, how you are showing up, and what is happening with your team, it is easier to act on it. Then you can work to create a team that is fulfilled and happy, nurture a company that is performing, and be a leader who takes ownership for your individual and collective growth. It all starts within. In this first section of the book, "Showing Up," I'll give you the steps and strategies required to look within yourself to show up as the leader you want to be. We'll explore the impact of building greater self-awareness and learning how to strategically execute your freedom and free will. You ultimately get to flip the script here and shape the team (and success) you deserve. This journey begins with truly considering some tough questions:

- *Do I want the team I truly deserve?*

- *Do I want to be fulfilled?*

- *Do I want to push my own boundaries?*

- *Do I want to ask things of myself that no other supervisor or leader has asked of me?*

- *Do I want to be able to work with my team in a way that I never have before?*

- *Do I want my team to be led in a way that they've probably never been led before?*

You can have it all, though you need to do the work, both on yourself and with your team. Success is an ongoing expedition that requires an understanding of your team, your climate, and your environment, along with your impact on each of them. What matters most is what lies on the deeper level of your desires, and that it is aligned with serving and elevating other people. When you take the initial steps to show up and start lovingly brushing away the brambles and clearing your meadow of all that is holding you back, you can start planting the seeds that give way to the greatest fruit— those of fulfillment, success in all facets of your life, empowered teams, and a thriving organization. Then, from that clear, gleaming meadow, you can wholeheart- edly welcome other weary travelers who happen along your way, helping to encourage them into the authentic, fully empowered leaders they are intended to be. The end result is that you get the teams that truly reflect all that you are putting in—the kind that are excited about everything from the big-picture mission to their daily tasks.

Let's dive in and explore how showing up with self-awareness, free will, determination, curiosity, and creativity will get you there.

BUILDING SELF-AWARENESS

GO WHERE THE SILENCE IS

Dig a little deeper and you'll see that everything becomes personal.

ARE YOU READY for that next step you seek in your career or within your organization? Do you have what it takes to be a truly great leader or CEO? Can you create the team of your dreams?

For as long as you can remember, you've wanted more out of life. From a personal standpoint, you may wish for success and longevity of that success. Chances are, however, that your goals are often outlined in statistical and monetary terms. From a business standpoint, you likely want what you were hired for or created your company for: to bring success to the organization, to make shareholders or investors happy, and to commit to environmental endeavors and community outreach. While none of these are negative things, are they a true depiction of what you really want?

Until now, your aspirations have likely been defined in terms of *results* you'd like to realize, and those results have likely been centered around business, but dig a little deeper and it's clear to see that everything you desire quickly becomes personal. It becomes about who you are as a leader and how that is impacting your team and the state of your organization. When your goals are defined after gaining full awareness of who you are, it changes the game and the conversation.

Most people start by setting their sights on what they want to have (the desired results) and drive forward from there. But fewer people will talk about the actions or behavior required to get the results they want, and fewer yet will talk about self-awareness, or what I call their State of Being, and what is required from within to elicit the behavior that will get the results. And yet this final piece is what produces the greatest, longest-lasting results! When it comes to going within yourself, into the silence, to help shape the success you desire, it can often feel easier to shy away from going there. Creating an internal state that will fuel your ultimate potential is indeed much harder work than simply focusing on the external. Yet it is also the only way to truly push the boundaries of what you believe is possible for yourself and your organization, allowing you to step into genuinely rewarding success.

In their March 2018 paper "Self-Awareness and Leadership: Developing an Individual Strategic Professional Development Plan in an MBA Leadership Course," researchers Arthur Rubens, Gerald A. Schoenfeld, Bryan S. Schaffer, and Joseph S. Leah of Florida Gulf Coast University reinforce the relationship between self-awareness and overall leadership success. Citing a 1993 study that reviews the causes of leaders' derailments, they note the four primary areas of leadership failure: interpersonal relationship problems, not meeting objectives, team leadership breakdowns, and inability to adapt to transitions and changes. As they point out, all four of these areas relate back to self-awareness, though they may be especially applicable to one's ability to adapt to change.[3] Your potential as a person and a leader begins with the pursuit of greater self-awareness and a willingness to grow into what you're being called to do.

STEP BACK (TAKE A SELAH SECOND)

INSIDE EACH CHAPTER that follows, you will be invited to "take a Selah Second." This is your opportunity to pause and consider the principle at hand. The Hebrew word *selah* is used at the end of certain verses in the Book of Psalms and has been interpreted to be about taking time to pause and calmly think about that which has come before. So carve out the necessary time and do your best to answer the questions in each of those sections. Consider both what has brought you to where you are and who you are today, and what you want to change to shape your longer-term legacy and impact.

In this Selah Second, sit in the silence and consider the following questions:

- *What is the best version of myself, and how do I identify and apply it authentically as a leader?*

- *How can I bring the best of myself to the table to elevate those around me?*

- *How can my own self-awareness and self-acceptance lead to greatness for my team and organization?*

- *What is the height of what we can realize when we shape our success from the inside out?*

As you ponder these questions, remember that "I don't know" is as acceptable an answer as any, because not knowing is a permission slip to lean in, learn, and grow. As a leader, you are likely looking for answers, because as you have already experienced, there are no smooth lines or straight paths to success! Not many leadership books will outright tell you that it's okay not to know exactly where you want to be or how you'll get there. Just the same, not many will encourage you to go within and learn the answers to these questions as you progress on your journey. This book will.

STEP INTO ACTION

IN THE THICK of daily challenges, unexpected circumstances, and the constant hustle of business, there is a magical thing called silence. Though it can be immensely challenging to notice, let alone seek out amid your daily bustle, you absolutely must, because the silence will become one of your biggest allies. By going there, and only by going there, will you fully expand your growth and define and hone the direction of your success. In the silence lies the opportunity to step up, realize your leadership, and express it at the highest level. In the silence lie the words not yet spoken, questions waiting to be asked, and puzzle pieces awaiting discovery. As you step into a space of questioning who you want to become as a leader, you are taking the first step of walking into that silence to find the answers you seek. By "not knowing" and "going there," you will also likely discover that you do in fact know the answers you seek, even if that awareness is buried many layers below the surface.

To help guide your moments of introspection, here are several actionable steps you can take:

1. **Recapture the Original Opportunity**

    Think back to when you were learning about and considering your current job. Remember the feelings associated with stepping into that role and how it felt when somebody saw you and gave you a chance. Now "re-give" yourself that original opportunity and step back into the feelings associated with it.

2. **Gather Your Keywords**

    When you look inside and think about what you are feeling in relation to a time (or the times) when you were welcomed into a great new role, which keywords come to mind? Write them down and internalize them.

3. **Pair Your Thoughts, Feelings, and Keywords**

    Align the thoughts, feelings, and keywords that have come to you in the first two action steps. Write them down and read through them. Now, with the sentiment of them top-of-mind, re-answer the aforementioned questions:

- *What is the best version of myself, and how do I identify and apply it authentically as a leader?*

- *How can I bring the best of myself to the table to elevate those around me?*

- *How can my own self-awareness and self-acceptance lead to greatness for my team and organization?*

- *What is the height of what we can realize when we shape our success from the inside out?*

Consider how you answered these questions earlier and how you answered them now. What has changed? Have your responses become elevated or clarified? If yes, how so?

You must be willing to go within and step into the silence to perform the necessary self-exploration to effect the highest levels of your leadership. This work is a courage workout sure to pay off. It will liberate you into free will and creativity, leading to a flywheel effect that can propel significant opportunity and achievement. It is in the contemplative and observant nature of going within that you will find your leadership voice in a way that allows you to boldly shape and say what others need to hear. To truly succeed, each one of us must embrace the silence and talk about the esoteric. More than focusing your career about what you want to do or have, leadership must become about who you want to *be*. The other results will follow when you are willing to dive within, reach beyond what you once knew to be possible, and challenge yourself to execute your day-to-day from a State of Being that empowers those you serve at a higher level. Then and only then can you discover the full potential and ultimate personal satisfaction of what you can truly "do" or "have."

May you run swiftly toward the silence, because when you do, you will open up a space in which to discover the wholeness of yourself, your authentic voice, and your leadership, along with the clarity of direction you seek—all the elements that will allow you to execute at the highest level with the teams you lead and the people you empower, each and every day.

DIVE IN, DIFFERENCES FIRST

You have the freedom to be who you are and to find success, not in spite of but because of your uniquely beautiful and powerful differences.

DO YOU EVER feel like a round outcast seated among a group of squares? It can be an uncomfortable existence, living and leading while trying to fit into someone else's square holes—expectations built, institutional frameworks formed, and systems shaped long before you arrived to take a seat at the table. Others may passionately want to make you fit into their definition of the world and freely offer insights as to the way business should be done and who and how a leader should be.

In business and in life, we don't meet strangers along the way; we are all strangers in a strange land. That said, our commonalities are still far greater than our differences. To one degree or another, we are all on a journey to realize personal satisfaction and success, and it takes a diverse group of individual leaders to build a stronger collective whole. You have unique gifts to share as a leader, just like everybody else. Diving in, differences first, means being able to look at yourself and what you bring to the party as *pluses*, not hindrances or things that you necessarily need to change; because as you are able to fully accept your differences as an integral component of your leadership, you begin to shape the truest, most authentic form of success, for your organizations, your communities, and yourself.

Growing up, I loved to play basketball. I truly admired the varsity high school team and their strong, winning tradition. I remember thinking, *I'm going to make the team*, even though I had little hope in actually making the cut. In the summer of my sophomore year, I was in the gym playing basketball by myself when the trainer of the varsity girls' team came in. He walked up and began to show me how to "shoot correctly." In those days, women only shot "the set shot," which was literally shooting from the hip. I was shooting above my head, like the men I watched play on television. As the trainer worked to correct my shot, the head coach came in and admonished him. Coach said, "Don't do that! Don't mess with her shot. She has a naturally high release."

Everything the coach said that day was a bit Greek to me at the time, but I'll always remember the next thing that came out of his mouth: "I'd like you to try out for the varsity team. Do you want to?" Did I want to?! Try out for a winning team with a history of excellence? A team that was cherished and held in high esteem by not just my school but around the league? A team whose members were seen walking the halls together and doing good things to help others, and always seemed the best of friends? Oh, heck yeah, I wanted some of that ... and I was also bloody terrified to do it. Other than a little "church ball" with my cousins at the YMCA, I didn't have any formal basketball skills or training. But just as Byron saw my potential as CEO many decades later, Coach saw my potential and embraced my differences as a gift to the team. What I lacked in skills that the other, more veteran players had, I made up for in passion, determination, and hard work. And of course, I was the only girl who shot like the boys. I joined the team and worked up to a starting position my senior year, when we became conference champs.

Sometimes the differences that "round you out" are what make you truly great. As you step into those leadership shoes that you have been asked to fill, or as you grow further into your current role, choose to see it as an opportunity to focus on what your differences are, how they contribute to your State of Being, and how you can use them to bring your best to every situation. Every one of your individual differences, quirks, and traits is potentially useful. They are all part of you, because you are an exquisite, powerful, worthy creation, made in God's image. God blesses everyone with the ability to bear good fruit, and our differences serve to strengthen our commonalities and our common goals.

When you can love yourself, then you get the opportunity to figure out who you are and bring *all* of that to the table. Every day, you can step deeper into awareness and acceptance of yourself and your differences. My high school varsity basketball coach saw potential in me and went out on a limb for this skinny kid with few skills and a lot of passion and willpower. He gifted me some of the best memories and experiences of my life— and yet make no mistake, I also had to work for them.

STEP BACK (TAKE A SELAH SECOND)

LONG AGO, MY mother gifted me a plaque carved with this powerful insight: *You are a unique individual, just like everybody else.* She instilled in me the value of our uniqueness as individuals and as leaders. What she shared bears repeating and remembering. Write down the following:

> *I am a unique individual,*
> *just like everybody else.*

Now write down some of the traits that make you unique and could be considered your assets:

> *What makes me unique is …*

STEP INTO ACTION

WHEN YOU EMBRACE them, your differences can fuel your desires and results in a uniquely powerful way. But the embracing process will come only through getting to know yourself. Remain open to having others help you in that process. Here are some steps you can take:

1. **Self-Observe to Gain Self-Acceptance**

   Spend time self-observing. Through the process, fold in self-acceptance as you go through the ups and downs of everyday business and life. Be vulnerable and transparent with yourself and others, and give yourself the space to say:

   - *I love myself.*
   - *I get myself.*
   - *I'm not beating up on myself anymore.*
   - *I'm not living in a state of delusion.*
   - *I'm not lying to myself (or to others).*

2. **Elicit Feedback**

   Communicate with your team to gain further awareness of your uniqueness, how others are receiving it, and how best you can bring all of yourself to work every day. Take the time, whether formally (with 180-degree feedback surveys) or informally (in conversations with your team), to ask where you are adding value and where things can be improved.

After my first year as CEO, and again two years later, I did 180-degree feedback surveys with my leadership team to learn how I was doing. I believed in the method and the value of the feedback. As it turned out, I was doing a better job than I gave myself credit for. My team members also reminded me to trust in myself! I was on the cusp of doing things right, and it was a perfect storm in the best kind of way.

Such 180-degree feedback surveys can be a great tool to identify both your unique competencies and any competency gaps. They can help you plan for your own development as a leader or for that of your team. They will also help improve your own awareness and appreciation of your unique capabilities and highlight areas of improvement. You must, however, be prepared for what you get back and ready to do something with the data, or you won't be helping anyone, least of all yourself.

When it comes to your differences, not everyone on the playground is going to get along; others won't always get you, and you most definitely won't always get your way. What's important is that you embrace your unique abilities and live powered by them. The journey of working to be truly confident with who you are and with the choices you make can be a long one, and it is one worth taking. Thriving as a unique leader living fully in your authenticity will inevitably involve a messy maneuver between staying true to who you are and dancing with what others are asking you to be. Sometimes you will be bumping along on an imperfect path with imperfect people, but you need to remember why you are in your role, and that you have the necessary potential, talents, and gifts to be there.

What matters most is that you know who you are and that you are bringing *all* of yourself to the table. Self-acceptance is paramount, and the aim should always be to become the leader you are intended to be. Because eventually, in that place where you are free to unapologetically be your best self, you will find your Zen. And then, and only then, can you become a celebrated and innovative leader who goes on to encourage the truths, differences, and unique traits of those around you.

SURRENDER TO NOT ALWAYS BEING RIGHT

*Acceptance is less about how others see you
and more about your willingness to say yes to
opportunities to become who you need to be.*

Do you sometimes struggle to find acceptance from others? Do you feel as though not everyone is listening or buying in to your visions the way you wish they would?

In every new adventure you take on, you will inevitably want to forge ahead with your intentions, while also being accepted. Yet some days you will try until you are blue in the face, only to have your efforts fail to get through or garner appreciation. You will say things to your team that won't land, you will mistakenly point fingers, or you will do things that leave fingers pointing right back at you. People may not love your suggestions on a Monday morning or your personality on a Thursday afternoon. There will also be times when the traits that make you different do not resonate with some people, or when you feel misunderstood or marginalized. While these may be warning flags that need to be followed as you dive deeper into awareness of your current state (of being), they can also be indications that it is time to step back, examine what you are doing, take the feedback given to you, and figure out whether you need to do things a new way. This concept can be shattering, as there is often a presumption that leaders have all the answers, but I ask you to remain humble and coachable.

Patrick Lencioni, a pioneer in the organizational health movement, is dedicated to changing the way we think about success and preparing ourselves for it. He is a corporate trainer and the author of eleven books, including *The Ideal Team Player: How to Recognize and Cultivate the Three Essential Virtues*. In his TEDx Talk,

"Are you an ideal team player?", Lencioni states that "life, more than ever, is a team sport." He also states, however, that in this "era of teamwork in business," we are often trained for "primarily individual and technical skills." In his talk, he outlines the three virtues of ideal team players, stating that the power of these virtues is in combining them—and that ideally, you need all three.

According to Lencioni, ideal team players are:

1. Humble. If you want to be an ideal team player and be successful in life, you really need to be humble. The antidote to pride is humility—putting others ahead of ourselves—though it must also come in conjunction with authentic confidence in ourselves.

2. Hungry. People who have an innate hunger to get work done are more successful; they go above and beyond, never doing just the minimum.

3. Smart. Being smart, Lencioni believes, is about "how we understand people and how we use our words and actions to bring out the best possible impact in others." Ideal team players have emotional intelligence.[4]

STEP BACK (TAKE A SELAH SECOND)

It can be all too easy to build up expectations about who you should be as a leader. A true leader is a true learner. When you feel you aren't being seen, heard, or understood as desired, it's important to stop and assess the situation. Where you have made a certain decision, you might find yourself questioning the "rightness" (or even righteousness) of it. When you think things should be happening differently, it is critical to pause and ask yourself this:

> *Do I want to help make things right,*
> *or do I need to always be right?*

Personally, there were points along my CEO journey where I had to choose between furthering my development and always being right. During those times when I felt convinced that something should be working (when it wasn't), I would stop the carousel, get off the horse, and go and talk to the stakeholders on the team responsible for getting the task accomplished. Much like the humble awareness that can come from the results of 180-degree feedback surveys, it can be enormously rewarding to take off the *it's got to be this way* gauntlet, stop pushing forward in relentless pursuit, and just talk. When I would ask my team why things weren't working and why we were having such a hard time achieving a goal, they would always have an answer that, when developed further, inevitably created a better way forward.

STEP INTO ACTION

IN ANY SITUATION, you can choose to grow or you can claim to know. When you show up with trust, support, transparency, kindness, and compassion (toward them and toward yourself), those you serve can see your authentic partnership with them. Doing so takes conscious action and continued self-awareness. Consider these steps you can take to guide your progress:

1. **Turn Outside Focus In**

   True leaders don't just push things ahead outwardly; they are willing to pause and change things within themselves. With so much going on inside your organization every day, it can be all too easy to forget to stop and look within—though in doing just that, you can move forward with more grace, humility, and fluidity.

2. Be OK with Not Knowing

We talked about this earlier, though it bears repeating: Where there is a problem, solution, or misunderstanding, give yourself permission to not know all the answers. No one ever said that leading was about always knowing. Be resourceful and stay humble as you seek out those who have the answers you may not.

3. Maintain a Childlike Curiosity

A sense of childlike curiosity is essential. Sometimes this also means stepping to the side, or to the back of the line, and observing rather than pushing your own personal agenda forward.

A sense of freedom and of awakening blossom simultaneously when you realize who you are, embrace your differences, and accept that you won't be everyone's Yoda mentor. People are not always going to like you, and sometimes it's not about being liked; sometimes it is simply about how you are interpreting someone or a situation, or how others are interpreting you. Maybe your calculations or expectations were off, and you have to be willing to take feedback to navigate or negotiate things a little better. A true leader knows that acceptance needs to be less about how you think your company, your boss, or the board should accept you, and more about your willingness to say yes to new opportunities to become how you need to be and then build the self-awareness required to get there. Be willing to evolve, to empower others, and to try doing things in a new way. And remember that despite the title of this book, sometimes when others don't like or agree with you, there is an element that is *not* about you. Sometimes it's just about the growth, dynamics, and selfless sacrifice required to become CEO.

It doesn't matter how high you ascend on the food chain; it's imperative that you remain coachable and humble. In every circumstance where you feel you are not being seen or heard, there's a valuable opportunity to learn a new lesson if you are willing to drop back, park the horses, start the campfire, and have the conversations with your team. As the leader, you get to ask, *What do you think we should do?* That single question re-empowers your team and allows those you serve to see you as a helper and a true leader. You are showing your team that you are in front of them but also beside them. Equal parts leader, learner, and partner.

A STATE OF BEING CAN SHIFT EVERYTHING

*Know how you are showing up, and you
will have the eyes to see where things
are going and to shift where needed.*

Do YOU WANT to create a great environment for others to work in? How about a thriving culture alongside great results for your company?

When you want to be, do, or have something, the question is always how much you are willing to work to have it. That's the behavior piece. The next layer then becomes who you need to be to get that behavior. That is where the real questions you need to be asking yourself come into play. In the initial chapter of this section, you read something that bears repeating: Most people start with the results they want and drive forward from there; fewer people dig a layer deeper and talk about the actions or behavior required to get the results they want; and even fewer investigate their State of Being and what is required from within them to elicit the behavior that will get the results. Yet this is the piece that drives the greatest, longest-lasting results.

State of Being > Behavior > Results
BEING > DOING > HAVING

State of Being is what I define as your mental, emotional, spiritual, and physical state. It is your platform of operation for absolutely everything you think, say, or do. Ultimately, your State of Being gets shaped by answering the question, *How do I show up authentically and bring the most value?*

In 2012, when Byron announced that I would be our company's next CEO, Hubert Joly had just taken over at the helm of Best Buy and was tasked with turning the company of 125,000 employees around. He quickly became one of my personal heroes. As an outsider coming in, Joly was handed an organization that analysts were predicting would go out of business or be taken apart by a private equity firm. With the imminent threat of a rapidly growing Amazon empire, Joly quickly went to work transforming the company, though he did so with a desire to create "human magic," which he defines as what happens "when at scale you have employees that do things for each other and for customers that nobody has told them to do."[5]

Joly described the philosophy behind Best Buy's resurgence as a decision to reshape the company to "pursue a noble purpose, put people at the center of the business, create an environment where every employee can blossom, and treat profit as an outcome, not the goal."[6] Joly chose to become aware of his company, his people, his competition, and himself at the deepest level, in terms of both where they were and where they needed to be. What he didn't yet know about the retail industry, he learned, putting himself on the ground floor at the company's store in St. Cloud, Minnesota. He wore the standard khaki pants and blue Best Buy shirt, with a name tag that read "CEO in training."[7]

Joly recognized that for Best Buy to stay afloat, the company and employees would have to realize the real needs their customers had and give them what they required. The staff would also have to "redefine who they were." In redefining themselves as "a company that's in the business of enriching lives through technology by addressing key human needs,"[8] they worked to create a greater level of care, enthusiasm, and purpose for the work to echo throughout the organization. And so under the umbrella of the turnaround strategy "Renew Blue," Joly and his team endeavored to educate and empower his people to deliver the highest levels of service. By the end of 2012, Best Buy announced that sales were flat and revenue declines seemed to be over. By 2016, the turnaround was complete, and Joly began spearheading the company's new mission of "Building the New Blue." What Joly did in his seven years with Best Buy was to change the company's State of Being—though it's more likely he changed the State of Being for himself first, then for the company. Today, the people of Best Buy are no longer in the stores simply to sell electronics, because Joly helped shape the heart of their business.

STEP BACK (TAKE A SELAH SECOND)

IN THIS SELAH Second, think about your day today. Where you may once have questioned results or behaviors, instead ask yourself:

How am I showing up today?

Keep asking *why* you are showing up as you are, and you will get to the root cause of your current State of Being. You can begin by looking at the results you are getting, then backtrack into behavior and the State of Being behind them. Make the choice to be aware of and shift your State of Being into one that is authentically aligned with your mission and the task at hand. Doing so will allow you to work from the root of any issue, in order to shift your results for the better. That said, while ongoing awareness is important in helping to monitor your State of Being, none of us are designed to be in a constant state of awareness. A team of MIT neuroscientists recently found that the human brain can process images that the eye sees for as little as 13 milliseconds, which is the first evidence of such rapid processing speed. Every second, our eyes receive 10 million bits of information for our brain to process from our external world, though our "intelligent" or "conscious" activities involve a processing capacity of only 50 of those 10 million bits per second![9] Life would be wholly overwhelming if we had to be aware of it all. Awareness of your State of Being should be a natural process, not an overwhelming venture.

STEP INTO ACTION

ANY OF US can become perceptive enough to know how we are showing up (or how we need to show up). To achieve the results and behaviors you want, begin by asking:

- *What's my State of Being?*
- *What does my State of Being need to be to get the desired behavior and results?*

If you aren't aware of how you are showing up, how will you know to alter your behavior and your actions to get the best results? Think about it. When you have a feel for your business, your team, and yourself, you can become perceptive enough to know how you are showing up and how you need to show up. With awareness of your State of Being, you have the eyes to see the direction things are going to go (good or bad) and how to shift where necessary to bring more of your natural self to the success of the whole. If there's a disconnect between your current State of Being and the one required to get the results, you'll need to adjust your State of Being. What that means is you'll need to show up differently, more authentically, and in closer alignment with your mission. Be thoughtful, do your pre-work, think about the meetings, bring the appropriate tools, and carefully consider what you want to convey.

It takes being fluid and flexible to fulfill a leadership role. Curiosity is key when it comes to having a feel for how you are showing up and being aware of when you need to make a dynamic shift to show up differently. On any given day, you will find yourself stepping forth with different States of Being that allow you to adapt to varying situations and conversations, and with members of your team. As you begin to understand that you have free will and choice to influence your own State of Being, that's where all of this gets traction. Address your State of Being, and you address the engine that will drive the choices and changes necessary to inform the behavior that will get the results you want and build the team you deserve.

FREEDOM AND FREE WILL

IT'S ALL ABOUT THE "WANT TO"

*To be, do, or have anything, you
need to have the "want to" first!*

IF YOU COULD do anything, what would you do? If you
could be anything, what would you be? Most people will
say they don't know the answers to these questions. If
that is your current thinking, then ask yourself: *If I did
know, what would the answer be?*

Free will is our God-given gift to make choices every day. It is a great empowering concept to help answer
the big questions, but it's one thing to say that you need
to focus on achieving your potential and it's another to
find the willpower and determination to forge ahead,
no matter how challenging the circumstances. Progress

will always require a fuel that powers you to transform free will into willpower. That fuel is what I call your "*want to.*" Your *want to* is your inner desire and drive to be, do, and have more. It is the connection between your passions, your desires, and your goals which, in turn, drive your behavior and actions. It is founded in a fierce sense of loyalty and dedication, and it is driven by grit and determination. Your *want to* serves as a reserve tank of energy that pushes you to reach a little further and push a little more in the pursuit of that something bigger that is fulfilling both your career success and your personal satisfaction.

You can *want to* ...

- Dig deeper.

- Do better.

- Be greater.

- Build a more empowered team.

- See your organization truly thrive.

While on an American Express members' tour of Napa Valley a few years back, I enjoyed spectacular dinners with winemakers and vineyard owners. One of the dinners landed us at the Mondavi home, where we ate in a picturesque ranch overlooking the vineyards with Angelina, Alycia, Riana, and Giovanna Mondavi. While many may glorify winemakers, these four sisters struck me differently. They were gracious, hard-working women who had made the choice to live in authentic alignment with who they were and what they wanted to do. Their great-grandparents Cesare and Rosa Mondavi bought Charles Krug Winery after the end of Prohibition and poured their passion, determination, and vision into a place that helped shape Napa Valley into one of California's premium wine regions. Their grandparents Peter Sr. and Blanche took over the winery operations in 1966, introducing revolutionary winemaking techniques that included cold fermentation, cold sterile filtration, and aging wine in French oak barrels. From the age of ten, the four sisters spent their summers learning the family business, and as adults the sisters chose to continue the family legacy. In 2005, they launched Dark Matter Wines, designing it to be far from traditional, though always in alignment with the mission of creating wines with the same passion and devotion as the generations before them. The four sisters are all involved in the company and share ownership. Alycia works on sales and marketing, while Angelina makes the wine, Riana (who also works for the family business at CK Mondavi) helps with sales, and Giovanna focuses on finance and social media.[10] Angelina Mondavi calls their winery "a nod to our family traditions with an edgy twist."[11]

Sometimes—as with the Mondavi sisters—your *want to* is undeniable, forged within you from an early age. You may honor and run with it, adding your own flair and uniqueness as you go. Sometimes, however, you may have a burning *want to*, and yet when you get into the weeds of it you realize it is not really what you actually want. I ran into this on my "professional climb." During the early stages of my nearly forty-year career in our family business, I had in my mind's eye what I thought I wanted: I was going to be sales manager, and then I was going to be CEO—then I hit my forties and everything changed. I felt stagnant and wanted nothing more than to be out of my family business. I explored new careers in my mind—from selling Doritos to becoming a park ranger—it was all on the table. Some people may have called this a mid-life crisis, but I chose to see it as a natural progression of simply being a human being. Eventually, I decided these other careers probably weren't my calling, and I moved over from sales manager and became our company's chief communications officer. The role was a need we had within the company, and it helped me learn how to work with many different people—from labor attorneys to the Equal Employment Opportunity Commission (EEOC), and from landlords to clients. It also provided the greater experiences and knowledge I would eventually bring to the CEO role.

Everybody has a *want to* within them; it is that part of you that wants to do and be more. But you have to get out of your own way to access it. You may also need to spend some time with that friend named Silence. When you are faced with situations like walking into a new role within an organization that has a crappy culture and having to clean things up, or finding yourself needing to take disciplinary actions or part ways with longtime employees, there has to be a *want to* if you're going to move forward. The same goes for being tasked with asking the hard questions within yourself or to (or from) those looking to you for leadership.

STEP BACK (TAKE A SELAH SECOND)

THERE IS FREE will in every choice you make. When you get up from where you are seated, you often quickly make the decision to move forward, go right, or go left. When you walk out of your office, you can decide to go for another cup of coffee, or you can decide to speak with a member of your team. It's up to you to be courageous and recognize opportunities to execute your *want to*. For the next hour, pause and be aware of all the times you feel you are in the presence of your *want to*. Write down your conclusions to the following statement:

*I am powerfully and positively
executing my free will when I …*

When it comes to exercising your choices, fear may creep in. If it does, acknowledge it while you stay true to your bigger mission and yourself.

STEP INTO ACTION

UNFOLDING YOUR *WANT to* is a metamorphic process of unpacking your ultimate desires. The discovery process can take time and work. It can also be a thorny journey, so you must have courage. It's about trying that "something else" in the face of failure. When you learn to say yes to your *want to*, you begin to foster and empower a similar drive in others, and lift them up in the process. The journey all begins with determining where your *want to* lives. There are two primary steps to this work:

1. **Making the Choice**

   Your *want to* isn't an automatic, knee-jerk response; it's a deep-from-within, bigger-than-you *YES!* to an opportunity or challenge that lies before you. Sometimes, we don't realize the opportunity for growth until someone presents it to us; though action will only come after we have chosen to make it. Choice is tied to free will, and free will always comes first.

2. Fueling Your Actions

Having made the choice to shape something greater for yourself and others, you can then empower yourself to embrace your *want to* with every ounce of your being. Then use that excitement and enthusiasm to fuel your behavior and actions going forward. Passion alone won't cut it; you need to have clear desires and goals as part of the package.

Finding your *want to* is never a one-time thing. Unfolding and honoring it is a process of unlocking your human potential, in the pursuit of fulfilling your career success and reaching the highest levels of personal satisfaction. With every opportunity you are offered (and the challenges that come alongside it), you get to choose if you want to leap fully in the direction of your *want to* even if you have to walk through the mud to get to the treasure. You will always have choices, and it is an evolutionary process to continue to widen your *want to*. Revisit it and refresh it often. Sometimes you will also need to take a time-out to reset and dream even bigger. It all comes back to knowing what you want to have, and then doing the work to be, do, or have what it is that you want. Everyone who likes basketball wants to be LeBron James, but not everybody is willing to do what LeBron James has had to do to get the results. A willingness to do the work is what matters most.

YOU CAN'T FAKE HUSTLE

*It's impossible to do what you need
to do well when you are busy doing
what you don't need to do.*

WHERE WILL YOU direct your efforts? What should you do or not do? Who needs to be there with you?

When there is something you want to be, do, or have, you are going to push to create it. As a leader in business, however, it's easy to get trapped in overthinking and overdoing, which can create a heavy strain on you. Yet the opposite—floundering in a state of disconnect and doing very little to adjust or align—can be equally perilous. There has always been great power in free will—the freedom to choose—though it is a power that must be used strategically. Free will is woven into every decision of your every day, and it needs to begin with knowing yourself, having clarity about where you want to go (or don't want to go), and doing what's necessary to get there.

Recognizing that you can't fake hustle is about understanding what it takes to show up in *your* job (fulfilling *your* role and doing *your* tasks) every day. It's also about knowing what it takes to do the proper prep work to accomplish what needs to be done. It means not trying to be all things to all people, or attempting to do everyone else's job while keeping the necessary big picture in mind. Free will is a wonderful tool, but you can't do what you need to do well when you are busy doing what you don't need to do! You may be caught up in the vortex of working "in the business" because you feel like you aren't really "working" if you aren't, but that's an illusion. Busying yourself with others' roles or being sucked into details can be a recipe for disaster and overwhelm. A fake hustle or busyness can cause you to become a task-oriented, transactional leader instead of a big-picture, transformational leader who has clarity of mission and direction.

I have a friend I just adore. We'll call him B. B is a wonderful person, with a big, beautiful, generous heart. He also used to suffer terribly from a case of "the busies." Busy B could often be heard saying, "I would love to, but I'm so busy!" or, "That sounds great, but I'm just too busy." One day, we were talking about his business when B shared the challenges he was having with growing one of his companies. (Ever notice how "business" and "busyness" are basically the same word, with the exception of one very important letter: Y. And *why* is exactly what we should be asking ourselves when we are "so busy"!). B wasn't sure whether he should keep one of his companies open or continue to chase new ideas for creating more companies. I shared with him the concept of the Buddhist "monkey mind," which occurs when our mind is unsettled, restless, or confused and therefore, cannot be relied on to steer us effectively. It is human nature to often struggle with our State of Being, especially in the hectic and relentlessly driving American culture. We can easily get sucked into working *in* our business instead of *on* our business, using the excuse of being too busy to let ourselves off the hook of considering the big picture—or, gasp, looking within ourselves. Busy B has since done great work in understanding how his State of Being informs his intentions, his drive, his actions, and his results. The work helped to clarify where he *really* desired to spend his time and energy. He now exercises his free will to pursue, with singular focus, a business opportunity to which he feels truly called. It is also the one he feels will best serve others.

I once saw a bumper sticker with the message "Jesus is coming. Look busy." I laughed out loud because of its unexpected nature and its tongue-in-cheek message. Oh, the sweet irony of thinking it's more important to act as if we are busy doing something than to just *Be*, especially in front of Him who "makes our joy complete" (John 1:1–4). The art of busyness and doing others' work can be a distraction, deterring you from something bigger that you know you need to do (and maybe don't want to do). It can also be an excuse you might not realize you are making for not taking the time to get to know yourself and focus on what needs to be worked on internally. A fake hustle can quickly become a tactical tool that aids and abets you in shying away from your own greatness and leading authentically.

Florida State University researcher Roy F. Baumeister states in his paper "Free Will in Scientific Psychology" that "to discuss free will in the terms of scientific psychology is to invoke notions of self-regulation, controlled processes, behavioral plasticity, and conscious decision-making."[12] From this perspective, free will, while still ethereal in concept, is not an illusion, but rather the result of your self-awareness and conscious choice. Having free will means operating from a place of clarity about who you are and where you are going, without being plagued by the excessive strain of overthinking. Interestingly, free will can both inform this awareness of who you need to be and distract you from continuous dedication to it.

STEP BACK (TAKE A SELAH SECOND)

As THE ADAGE goes, "Exponential growth cannot happen with incremental thinking," and incremental thinking is what makes you busy, by putting you in positions three rungs down. Take a moment to look at the schedule for your last workday. As you revisit each task, ask yourself the following questions:

- *Was this task mine to complete?*

- *Did it involve incremental or exponential thinking?*

- *How can I change things for the better, starting tomorrow?*

STEP INTO ACTION

BEFORE YOU EXERT free will to do all things and be all things for your team, you need to identify *what it is that you need in order to do your job* and what it is *not* your job to do. Otherwise, you'll end up spending your days in directionless hustle and wear yourself out trying to do it all.

Three key steps will help you identify what you need to be doing:

1. Know What *Your* Job Is

In your heart, you are a problem solver. You climbed the ladder by doing a lot of fixing along the way, but you should be in charge of a company or team only if you know how to empower others and lead others—and that means not do-ing their jobs. It's time to look at your role as a CEO or leader as that of a champion for your team, to empower them to do their jobs.

2. Know What You Have to Do and What You *Don't* Have to Do

Only with clear direction on what you do and don't have to do can you begin to awaken and exercise strategic free will. Set clear objectives and tasks within your role. You will know that you are too deeply in the busyness of the busi-ness when you are doing all the talking in the meetings or trying to take care of the small de-tails of your direct reports' work. Do only your job, and let others do theirs.

3. Check in with Your State of Being

Free will is the essence of your State of Being. Ask yourself if you are currently caught up in a directionless hustle, or being strategic and au-thentic in your every action. Awareness of your State of Being (and authenticity as a leader) will help quell the "monkey mind" and aid you in identifying what you need to (not) be doing. It will also enable you to engage that awareness, which informs presence in every moment, and which is the best place from which to launch desired behavior.

Becoming accustomed to free will being a part of your days will feel much like getting used to the sense of driving at a certain speed in your car. When you have your destination and route clearly in mind, you don't have to constantly glance down at the odometer, because you know how a certain speed *feels* (remember that good ol' gut check?). As you get in your groove, you will also gain an instinct about when you need to rev up the RPMs and when you need to slow down. Where the rubber meets the road is when you must make choices in the heat of the moment, or when you haven't had enough sleep, or where there is no clear right or wrong, black or white, and you are swimming in a sea of gray. We will address these situations in more depth later in the book, but for now, keep asking yourself: *What is the behavior needed to get results, which are measured by the metrics?*

Free will is about much more than averting busyness or knowing what you need to do in order to do your job, because none of the choices and decisions you make will be as relevant if you aren't clear on the big picture of where you want to go. Free will and freeing yourself from the fake hustle all come down to clarity of decision and conscious choice along the way. Finding your groove in an energy-building hustle with a clear objective means being strategically busy, doing things that align with your role and who you authentically are. It's about aligning outward actions with your State of Being. This is where grit, determination, and resiliency live. Destiny is great, and following a calling is great, but a strategic hustle gives you the muscle and the stick-to-it-ness to focus, finish the mission, and get the desired results. That means operating from a constant state of mindfulness, and remaining open to shifting how you go about solving a challenge, while being pragmatic in getting done what needs to get done on a daily basis.

CHARISMA STARTS, AUTHENTICITY CLOSES

Leadership is about creating a sacred space
for others to step into their authentic selves.
It takes an authentic leader to do so.

ARE YOU TREATING others the way they need to be treated? Are you regularly building up your team? How are you treating yourself along the leadership journey?

Charisma can be a pinch hitter to fall back on when it is time to light the fire again, but nothing can take the place of transparency—of being true to yourself and sharing your authentic ideas toward solutions and moving the needle. You can't live and die on charisma, but you can step out onto the invisible bridge if you are transparently yourself. The role of a leader is nuanced and complex, and can vary greatly from day to day. Challenges and opportunities will require ongoing adaptation and readiness to engage. They will also ask very different things of you, so you need to work to stay aligned with your State of Being and bigger mission at every moment. And the only way to prepare for the next turns in the road is by being an authentic leader.

Billionaire Warren Buffett has spent the last five decades running Berkshire Hathaway Inc. The May 2021 *Wall Street Journal* article "Warren Buffett Says Bad Leaders Pose Biggest Risk to Companies" outlines Buffett's belief that "choosing the wrong people to lead an organization is the No. 1 risk for businesses." In his words, "You get a guy or a woman in charge of it—they're personable, the directors like 'em—they don't know what they're doing. But they know how to put on an appearance. That's the biggest single danger."[13]

If you execute free will without awareness of your State of Being and alignment with your authenticity, things can end up like a train on cruise control, running full speed off the tracks. You can try to fool yourself that you are going to slip something past your team, but grown-ups know! News will break that the caboose is lying on the side of the tracks. Those you lead are perceptive human beings with their own experiences, and they will surely know when you are being inauthentic or trying to put one over on them.

During my Executive MBA, we were taught that charisma was an important ingredient in being a successful CEO, but as we've noted, charisma will get you only so far. It can help you quickly get on board with your leadership team, their teams, your employees, and your clients, but what gets you to the party won't necessarily get you into the family or help you build long-term relationships grounded in trust and respect. At some point, you have to enter into the hard conversations, share principles and ideas, and learn what others think. Charisma in itself is not a bad thing, but leadership is ultimately about creating a sacred space for those you work with to step into their authentic selves, and it takes an authentic leader to do so.

The term "authentic leadership" was popularized by former Medtronic CEO and Harvard Business School professor Bill George with the release of his 2003 book by the same name. To help organizations emerge from the "corporate crisis," he called for a new type of leader, one dedicated to a mission-driven company rather than one that is solely financially driven.[14] His work has since become a gold standard for what authenticity in leadership can be and the positive impact it can have.

When it comes to authenticity, it's important to note that this is a socially constructed principle. In the 2005 *Harvard Business Review* article "Managing Authenticity: The Paradox of Great Leadership," London Business School emeritus professor Rob Goffee and his co-author, Gareth Jones state that "authenticity is largely defined by what other people see in you and, as such, can to a great extent be controlled by you. If authenticity were purely an innate quality, there would be little you could do to manage it and, therefore, little you could do to make yourself more effective as a leader."[15]

STEP BACK (TAKE A SELAH SECOND)

YOUR TEAM WILL be looking to you for direction and guidance. You cannot be authentic without knowing who you are, where you stand, and where you want to go! As a CEO or leader, your authenticity also stems from being confident that you are in your role for a reason. You didn't just stumble into a room and force yourself into the role; your credentials were good enough to get you hired! Have confidence in that. Everything you have done and all the uniqueness you have amassed has led you to this position. Once you can accept that you are there for a reason, it's important to also be compassionate with yourself and understand that building confidence takes time. Take a few minutes to write down your answers to the following questions:

Am I leading from my authentic self? If not, what would doing so look like?

STEP INTO ACTION

FOCUS AND FINISH: These two activities must be top of mind when you wake up every day, ready to exert your free will authentically. You got to where you are because you are very self-motivated. Reminding yourself to *focus and finish* may seem like a given, since remaining true to your authenticity amid challenges requires steadfastness. Focusing and finishing is about making the choice to focus on what you are *supposed to be* focusing on, driving forward, and finishing. In "You Can't Fake Hustle," you learned that before you can exercise free will, you need to hold yourself accountable for what *your* work is and what *their* work is. Now looking at the bigger picture, here are two ways to check in with yourself to ensure you are executing your leadership authentically:

1. **Prep Work**

    So much of being a leader lies in the prep work, along with staying in the orbit of awareness of yourself (your State of Being) and what is going on around you (your environment). Preparation begets awareness. Every Sunday, mindfully prepare for your week. Free will dictates that you can do anything, so you want to be sure to align your every action with your authenticity and what is required of your leadership. Prep work creates intentionality and provokes confidence that you will know the right thing to do to create the desired behavior and results, regardless of what comes your way.

2. Gut Checks

Sometimes you may feel that you *want to* do it all! Authentic leadership involves the ability to identify what it is that truly requires your attention by checking in with your gut. That said, none of us needs to become robotic about when and how to exercise free will. When you get too rigid with yourself, you get too rigid with your team. Go with the flow and constantly check in with your gut to see how things *feel*. Do a "gut check" on any circumstances to determine whether they are where you need to focus your energy.

As a leader, the most important area for you to *focus and finish* is your relationships. Where charisma can feel energetic and inspiring, authenticity provides the longevity of a grounded nature and clear direction. When it comes to executing free will to achieve authentic leadership, there is no silver bullet guaranteed to work for everyone in every circumstance. What matters most is figuring out who you are, pausing when you need to reset and execute free will that aligns with your authenticity. Times will change, your business needs will change, and your State of Being will change; what matters is that you are always being authentic, because when you are, your team will respect you and come to know you for it.

BE A DISRUPTOR, NOT A FLAMETHROWER

Sometimes the best thing you can do
to make things better is to rethink
them rather than redo them.

WHEN THINGS AREN'T going right, is your initial instinct to blow them up or to build them to be better? Do you act with quick fixes or step back and become strategic?

Many CEOs or leaders get hired to clean up a mess or fix something. You may arrive with your tool bags from other jobs, or else come from an operations or finance background and start trying to apply that to your new leadership role. While you may have walked in with a particular tool bag, expecting to be able to "plug and play," you may quickly discover that things that worked for you in a previous role or with a previous company are not working now. The situation can become overwhelming if you find yourself continuously putting out fires or unintentionally creating them. When rushing just to check all the boxes every day, you won't feel you have time to be creative or curious about how to truly make things better. In these situations, trying to regain the status quo can feel like a major challenge in itself.

One of my professional role models, British-American banking executive Jane Fraser, took over as Citigroup's first female CEO in March 2021. She walked into a real mess at the height of the global pandemic. On top of years of mismanagement and an underperforming stock value, deal volume was at record high levels, causing employees to face overworking during a time when pandemic burnout was already very real.[16] A seventeen-year veteran of the company, Fraser knew the corporate values well, though she also wasn't afraid to stand for something new. Less than a month into her new role, she initiated "Zoom-free Fridays," strongly encouraged employees to avoid scheduling calls outside traditional work hours, and emphasized the need for everyone to take their allotted vacation time. Then she did something beyond what would be considered commonplace in the financial world (outside of the pandemic): She decided after the pandemic that most roles at Citi would become hybrid—three days working in the office and up to two more working at home. She branded Citi as "a bank with soul." Her reason? Protecting the emotional and mental well-being of Citi's employees.[17]

There are plenty of reports of CEOs and business leaders who think that reaching their creative potential means destroying what currently exists. These so-called flame throwers are adept at blowing things up and being hard on their people. Most are control-oriented, type-A people whose MO is to engage in destruction and/or reconstruction. They are focused on checking all the boxes, and they have a high risk tolerance of which they often take full advantage. Yet changing things dramatically and continuously can quickly cause unwelcome disruption, which risks drawing attention away from the matters that require attention most.

For twenty-five centuries, the Acropolis in Athens, Greece, had undergone serious and continuous deterioration from fires, explosions, and earthquakes. Then in 1975 the Committee for the Conservation of the Acropolis Monuments was established to systematically restore the Greek structures by stabilizing, conserving, and prolonging the life of both the Acropolis and the Parthenon. Supervised by the Greek Ministry of Culture (which was in charge of coordinating, directing, and studying the renovation) and the Committee for Conversation, the restoration focuses on restoring the buildings spread around the Acropolis and piecing them back together while using new materials as sparingly as possible.[18] There is something important to be learned here.

No one wants to re-engineer a tried-and-true piece of history to the point of losing essential foundational knowledge. Modernizing is important, and we must stay abreast of things, but you also don't have to be forever reinventing the wheel. Sometimes it comes down to being willing to adapt. When Citigroup's Jane Fraser noted that not all workers were excelling while working remotely, she called those who were underperforming back into the office for coaching.[19] Being a disruptor, not a flame thrower, is about keeping the DNA of your organization intact while making positive changes for the better. You don't need to tear the whole structure down to the foundation and redo the rest to ensure that what you have is viable.

STEP BACK (TAKE A SELAH SECOND)

WHEN YOU OVER-ENGINEER things, not only is it harder to make them work, but then when they don't work, it becomes harder yet to figure out just why they don't—no matter how curious you are. In most cases, all that may be required are small strategic tweaks or a rethinking of what already exists. I've never flown an airplane, but the concept is fascinating to me—the ability to sail through the sky and arrive at your destination, all the while making small corrections as you go. That said, small changes can sometimes be harder to make than bigger overhauls, because they require you to be more thoughtful (versus pushing the plunger detonator). In order to ensure you stay on course toward your highest potential and success, in those situations where you feel tempted to blow things up, ask yourself:

> *What small corrections can I make*
> *instead of taking things apart?*

STEP INTO ACTION

As a leader, it is human nature to face times when you have a crisis of confidence or fall into knee-jerk reactions or old patterns based on how you yourself were managed. Having free will means that you understand that things are not destined for destruction and full reconstruction. There will inevitably be times when you need to shake up the status quo in order to make things better. In these cases, Strategic Disruption is required. True disruptors are strategic—they focus on the details that have a big impact in achieving alignment, or realignment, with the mission and values.

Here are some steps you can take to ensure you remain a Strategic Disruptor:

1. Make Pondering Your Best Friend

Before you step in to act, step back to ponder. Letting your mind roam can help you start to connect the dots and open up possibilities of new areas of exploration and expansion, or areas that need deeper, more hands-on involvement. Create space to contemplate what you perceive to be a challenge and how you are considering approaching it. Allow empathy, creativity, and outside-the-box thinking to become part of every equation.

2. Use Your Perspective for Good

Sometimes you don't want to risk watering down a conversation by passing it through various levels of the organization. On occasion, CEOs do need to go in and help those working at various levels of the company who may be outside their direct reports. People in your organization who are head-down, elbows-up, driving things forward for the organization every day may have the opportunity to notice what others often don't, because they are entrenched in the daily grind. You get to be a CEO or leader because you are an excellent problem solver and can see the bigger picture. Pondering helps you see these opportunities, and free will lets you step into them to ask the important questions and have the real conversations—disruption in its best form.

Checking all the boxes or hitting the giant metaphorical *delete* key isn't enough when you are aiming to be a good or great CEO operating with both self-awareness and free will. You don't need to rework everything every time. Disruptive thinking, in the most positive and progressive way, involves being willing to rethink things. Sometimes the most important action you can take is to just sit down with people and have a one-on-one, heart-to-heart conversation. You also want to help others feel confident that they can have an open and honest dialogue to solve problems, without their commitment to your corporate mission and values being disputed. Help them feel safe, seen, and cared for, as you let the flames of great challenge become a catalyst to gain clarity of what is truly relevant.

There are always two driving forces from which you can operate: one fueled by faith, trust, kindness, mercy, and grace; the other by fear, lack, disgrace, and harsh words and actions. Whichever of these forces you choose, the associated qualities will fuel your team, your company, and yourself. Choose the former, and you set the foundation to help ensure that you, your team, and your organization step progressively forward in a positive direction, toward their greatest potential. Like a watchmaker, focus on the intricate details that make the mechanism as a whole run effectively. One little thing that is out of sync doesn't mean the whole watch is broken. It is on you to be attentive, always acting in alignment with your mission and values, while remaining respectful of your team's hearts and minds. Stand tall in that vision, and don't allow it to be broken down by blowing things up. Then step in and help make a strategic difference with your disruption, and step out again after you have helped empower others.

II.
STEPPING INTO YOUR POTENTIAL

Realizing the full potential of who you are meant to be requires a solid foundation. This means strategically executing the unique behaviors that lead to desired results.

DOING THE WORK TO STEP INTO YOUR POWER

You can delegate the work, but you can't delegate the responsibility.

WHAT HAVE YOU done today to help others become the best they can be? What have you done to foster your own personal potential?

As CEO, you are ultimately responsible for pretty much everything. If you are going to be a great leader, you need to have a sense and understanding of your own power and your own personal work, as well as an understanding of just what is going on in your company and your teams. You can delegate the work, but not the ultimate responsibility. The truest definition of "it's on you" is about accepting the role and ultimate accountability for what you and everyone in your organization can become—your collective potential. But as a CEO or leader, you won't want to just walk into an organization with a new fifteen-year vision on day one. You must carefully gauge the rollout of your new ideas, goals, and metrics, while simultaneously running the company. You can share your ideas for the company, but take care not to overwhelm your team or yourself. You need to allow yourself time and room to grow.

Renowned speaker and author Brené Brown, who holds the Huffington Foundation Endowed Chair at the University of Houston's Graduate College of Social Work, has spent two decades researching courage, shame, empathy, and vulnerability. In a *Tonight Show* interview, when Jimmy Fallon asked her how she defined a leader, Brown said, "I define a leader as any person who holds themselves accountable for finding the potential in people and processes, and [who] has the courage and guts to develop that potential."[20] Stepping into your potential is about being willing to get up each day, have a shower, put on your clothes, and go bravely forward asking how else you can live into your calling, lift others up, and realize your own personal potential while doing so.

In the "Showing Up" section of this book, we looked at how you can build greater self-awareness and execute strategically on your free will. Now, it's time to consider the daily actionable behaviors that you can take to create the success and results you desire. We'll also look at the key roles that curiosity, creativity, care, and determination play in this journey. It's time to execute the strategic behaviors and actions that set creative thinking, determination, free will, and awareness in motion. As you move through your days, you can choose to see things through the lens of potential and ask yourself these questions:

- *What can I learn to be the best CEO I can be?*

- *What can I teach to help foster potential within others?*

- *Which principles can I adopt to create the best organization I can lead?*

This section delves into the behavioral steps required to "do your very best every single day," as the late

Colin Powell defined leadership. The former US secretary of state, US Army general, national security advisor, and chair of the Joint Chiefs of Staff addressed the key role played by potential when he said, "Leadership takes you farther than management thinks you can go. And you get that by inspiring people, by taking care of them. You give them what they need to get the job done, building confidence and trust with them, and they with you. And that creates perpetual optimism—it's a force multiplier, meaning it makes your force more powerful than the design of the force would suggest it is."[21]

In a 2018 interview with Whitworth University's *Whitworth Today* magazine, Powell spoke about his diverse scope of leadership learning and how he benefitted from good and bad advice alike, as well as the thirteen rules of leadership he came to stand by. The rules from his list that hit home the most for me are:

- It can be done.

- Be careful what you choose: you may get it.

- Check small things.

- Share credit.

- Remain calm. Be kind.

- Don't take counsel of your fears or naysayers.

- Perpetual optimism is a force multiplier.[22]

When I read Powell's thirteen points while working as CEO of Tipperary, I immediately had to share them with my team. Those you lead will encounter successes, failures, and more successes. There is no silver bullet, and you won't have all the answers. What you can do is celebrate the wins alongside them, and when they fail, act in ways that help them pick up the pieces and strategically rebuild to rise stronger. You can nurture all the people on your team as you strive to continuously grow. But you must be willing to put in the work, because potential is not some golden, glistening door that will magically fly open one day. It is a stair-step journey of navigating the real-life bumps in the road and strategically finding a way to come out stronger together. We are talking real inside-out change for the collective betterment ... all while aligning with the values that are critical to every one of us realizing our potential, namely:

- **Discipline.** In business, attaining your collective potential won't come with the snap of a finger. It requires strategy and steadfast dedication to doing your absolute best, no matter what every day holds.

- **Inspiration.** When the going gets tough, you'll need something to keep you going! Stepping into your potential and serving others in realizing theirs requires that you have accomplishments to fuel your quest. These may come from others, or they may be realized by looking back at what you and your team have already overcome and achieved.

- **Focus.** It is very difficult to reach a target that isn't clearly set in your mind's eye. Stepping into your collective potential also requires maintaining a consistent focus on your mission, values, and State of Being (how you are showing up). Are they supporting what you and your company want to become?

- **Belief.** Belief in yourself, your team, and your mission is critical to progress. This means being able to visualize the successful completion of the initiative and fulfillment of the target you had in your mind's eye.

- **Perseverance.** No matter what each day, month, or year brings, reaching for your potential necessitates that you continue to move forward with an attitude of believing you are going to get through it. This applies regardless of whatever "it" is, and however long it takes—bumps in the road, messy maneuvers, tough conversations, and all.

- **Agility.** While you seek progress, you must move with agility. Critical thinking is vital, but be prepared to adjust in the moment. Doing so helps you form situational awareness and see other potential avenues to success.

- **Creativity.** Imminent obstacles are sure to appear along the way, but you can still make the space and time to allow creativity into the problem-solving equation.

- **Care.** Potential can't be realized when a leader doesn't care enough to help everyone get there. Above all, it is imperative that you are aware of, care about, and have empathy for the people and issues facing your organization each and every day.

Stepping into your power and potential is a "both/ and" scenario. It's on you to take the actions that will help you rise into your own potential, while honoring your ultimate responsibility for everything within the organization. At the same time, through coaching, you are helping others reach *their* potential by ensuring that they are learning, growing, striving, and feeling satisfied. Although exactly how you and your team step into your potential is ultimately on you, you can establish a mutually beneficial leadership style. That's what this "implementation" phase of the book is about—the actions you can take on a daily basis to fuel continuous growth for all involved. You can prepare for change, but you can't control it. Through your behaviors and actions, you have the opportunity to give the members of your team and organization something they'll remember for the rest of their lives: support and love—all while managing the day-to-day business.

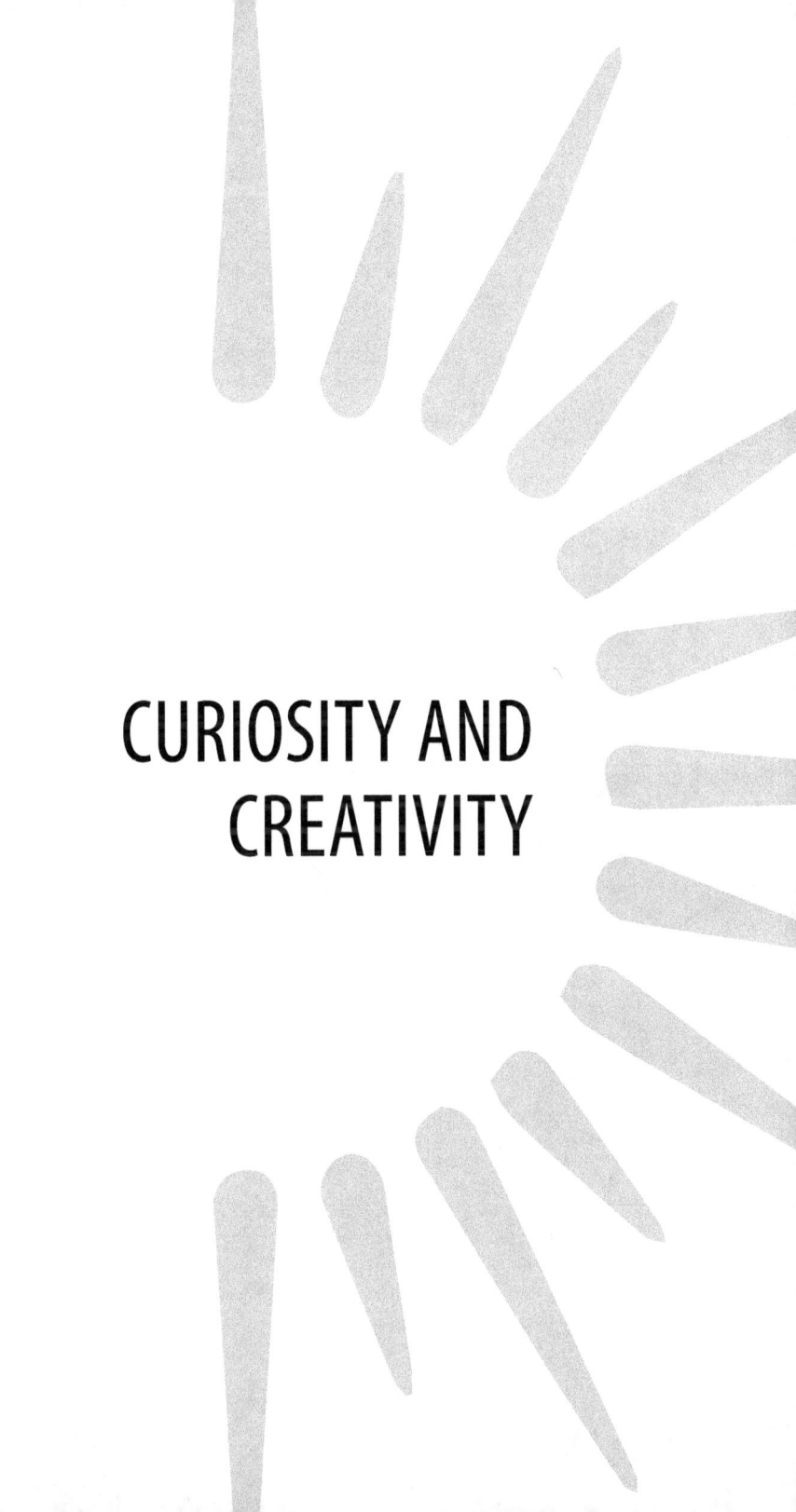

CURIOSITY AND CREATIVITY

ASK JUST HOW GREAT THINGS CAN BE

*Curiosity becomes the baseline
and fuel for everything.*

WHAT WOULD HAPPEN if you tried C, D, or even E, instead of the typical A or B? How would things look if you opened up further curiosity about just how great your life, business, relationships, and dreams can be? Would you start to see things differently? Could you start to believe that situations didn't always have to be messy struggles? Could there be greater ease? Greater potential?

Something is going to take shape, so why not create what you want and have things be as great as they can be? Better leaders have an innate sense of wonder about just how successful and just how awesome things can become, as well as just how great their team can be. They have a desire to mesh or align things better within a department, to problem-solve at the highest level, and to collaborate to create something better together. They are always asking questions and making sure they aren't missing something. None of this is possible without curiosity—the baseline and fuel for everything. Curiosity is the hunger, the thirst, the lying awake at 2:00 a.m. thinking about a problem because you know there's a better way to solve it. Equally important as spotting the threats from up in the metaphorical fire tower, big-picture curiosity can lead to previously undiscovered opportunities and solutions. As a State of Being, curiosity equates to continuous education that becomes the basis of your personal journey, your success, and the success of your team.

At one point, while I was CEO at Tipperary, we were struggling to make things work with one of our high-level positions. As much as we tried, it became clear that we had the wrong person in the seat. A deeper dive into their values and drive revealed that not only were they in the wrong seat, they were on the wrong bus! In his #1 bestselling book, *Good to Great*, global leadership teacher Jim Collins promotes the principle "first who, then what." In his words, you have to "get the right people on the bus," because "if you begin with 'who' rather than 'what,' you can more easily adapt to a changing world."[23]

Interestingly, we had another person within the organization who we felt was on the right bus but needed a change of seat. The issues surrounding the need to part ways with the high-level person were deep and often complex, but one day I had to draw a line in the sand. Interestingly, when we interviewed the "right bus" person to fill the high-level position, not only did they tell us that they would love the role but in the same breath, they also asked us if it would be okay to roll out improvements they had envisioned. Moreover, they also had someone in mind for the role they just left.

My seasoned inner critic was skeptical that things could work out so magically after all we had been through to get everyone into their best seats. One thing was certain, though: Everything the "right bus" candidate brought forth resulted from their lying awake thinking about how great things could be. Their enthusiasm and prior experience at the company came shining through in every suggestion. Initially upon landing the role, they made a few tweaks to improve things, though their ultimate vision and commitment to greatness were much larger. It was about more than just how great their position could be; it was about how great their entire department could become, and how committed they could be to their personal development! They wanted to continuously make things better for the department and the entire company. They were ready to have skin in the game, and this passion meant they ended up being the perfect person for the role. Their impact became so substantial and tangible that it even made me look at things in a new light, asking just how great their position could be. As CEO, I said yes to most of their ideas and offers, allowing them to lead the way to greatness.

If you are not curious, you are not moving forward to create something better. When you are curious, you continuously want to answer the question *How great can things get?* (the curiosity piece), followed by *How do we get there?* (the creativity piece). Curiosity and creativity are partners in success; they marry each other and feed off each other. Curiosity is the driver for remaining open to creative ways of doing business. That might mean problem-solving, goal creation, or the reworking of certain elements of your business, if that's what needs to happen. However, the buck stops with culture. Being curious is not enough to fuel success; if you have a crappy culture, it is hard to think bigger and solve better. You need to be hiring people who are also curious and hungry—the natural problem-solvers who are also lying awake at 2:00 a.m. wondering how to make things better. If you are spending time thinking about how elevated your leadership team could be with different people in place, it may be time to make some changes.

STEP BACK (TAKE A SELAH SECOND)

WHILE THIS CHAPTER is about asking how great things can be, our dreams can only become reality with the right people in the right places. If you could positively alter your expectation of what "good," "great," or the best possible CEO you can be look like, how would things evolve? Would what you envision as possible if you altered the most important things? Asking these questions may lead to your uncovering answers that vary drastically from your initial perceptions.

Start by asking yourself:

- *How would I rate my current "CEOness" (or leadership)?*
- *What can I do to help our organization rise from good to great to our best?*

In this process, you can also address all the armor someone else has given you—whatever may be holding you back from acting from your full curiosity and creativity. Shed that encasement in order to step more fully into your own greatness, so that you can help your team do the same.

STEP INTO ACTION

CEOs AND LEADERS are often guilty of missing opportunities because we are caught in the "busyness hustle," doing something else. Complacency (which for CEOs often means being busy doing something other than what you really need to be doing) and curiosity cannot occupy the same space. Here are some powerful points to help you stay curious and push yourself to and beyond your perceived limits.

1. Give Yourself Space

Allow yourself the time and permission to be curious in business. Looking at your schedule, you might think that finding time to be curious and creative is hard, but curiosity is critical to moving forward. It is vital for changing culture, getting the right people on board, and having the team you deserve. On occasion, you may have to condense your curiosity time, but it is a necessary ingredient in your problem-solving and strategic thinking, and you need to make time for it. Schedule it in.

2. Set Aside Old Tapes

The pursuit of greatness requires that you shine a light on the skeletons in your closet—the ghosts of your past that are haunting you, or antiquated corporate ways that are holding you back and no longer serving your organization. Seeing the potential of how great things can be will come only when you set aside the old tapes and burdensome thoughts playing over in your head, along with preconceived notions and self-defeating prophecies. What are the stories you've been telling yourself for too long now? It's time to give those stories less power and create a new way—one where curiosity and possibility reign.

3. Visualize

Step back from where you are and visualize what things would look like if the puzzle piece you are struggling with changed for the better. As CEO, I would spend a lot of time thinking about what things could look like if we improved situations where we had weak leadership or poor collaboration. Once you've visualized where you can be, visualize the steps you are going to take to get there. Then step into action and go do it!

Curiosity is ultimately about challenging your thinking and your willingness, but remember: It should be a fun, positive experience. Being curious should never invoke a level of stress that leaves you feeling you're ready to break in half. If it's worrisome or heartbreaking, it's not curiosity—or there might be a bigger picture to look at, like you possibly not being in the right role, company, or place. There will always be fires for you to fight, but you have to honor space for curiosity to keep yourself, your team, and the mission refreshed ... because only then will you have the eyes to see how truly great things can be.

ALLOW BUSINESS TO BECOME MORE CREATIVE

Often underconsidered, creativity can quickly become a game changer in business.

IN THE PAST day, how many times have you had to solve a problem? If options A and B weren't going to work, what did you do? Was your next step to use your curiosity to think of a new way to solve that problem? What could become possible if your next move was to step into your curiosity?

In a world where priorities and planning constantly need to change to keep pace, creativity in business is something that is often underdeveloped, underdiscussed, and underconsidered—yet when factored into your strategic business equation, it can quickly become a game changer. There is power in positive thinking and visualizing outcomes as part of the recipe for success. There is strength in saying you are going to do something or create something and having it in your mind's eye before seeing it through to completion. So often in business, we don't think about curiosity or creativity. I would like to give you a reason to think about them, because creativity is around you every day, and as a creative leader, when you employ it you can better ride the waves of ambiguity, solve problems, and seek new ways of doing things. You can solve problems creatively by thinking of new opportunities and challenging your own thinking (and maybe that of others). That is what this section on allowing business to become more creative is all about.

Before any doubt creeps in and you begin to question whether you can be creative, ask yourself how you think you've gotten this far. If you don't consider yourself creative, that might simply be because you haven't been encouraged to do so or have had some failed attempts. This is a good-news story, so surprise, I've got some more of it: If you have ever successfully solved a problem, congratulations—you're a creative person. If you have ever visualized yourself assuming a new role, buying a new house, or taking a dream vacation, you were being creative. When you become aware of how many times you've successfully solved problems in a twenty-four-hour period, you start to rethink what creativity can be. You also start to see its importance in your daily decision-making and goal-setting, as well as in your efforts to overcome obstacles. You then give creativity greater value and allow it the breathing room it requires to grow into a bigger, more influential role in your daily business.

On May 27, 2013, Mikael Cho founded photography site Unsplash by uploading ten photos to a Dropbox link. The company was built out of a desire to offer something more than expensive, cheesy stock photos. Mikael teamed up with a local photographer to create their first few custom images. At the time, Cho was the cofounder of Crew, an online marketplace for hiring freelance creatives, but Crew was struggling, with only three months of cash left and no venture-capital funding in sight. Cho knew he had to do something creative and new to keep Crew afloat.[24] He attracted attention by setting up a $19 Tumblr theme and giving images away for free, figuring his existing market could use them. He officially launched on Hacker News and was voted the top story. Within a matter of hours, Unsplash was officially born, and Cho's side project—one he designed to creatively meet the need to attract more clients to Crew with unique stock images—had drawn in 50,000 visitors in a single day. Within four months, Unsplash helped Crew double its revenue and secure $10.6 million in funding, and Unsplash soon became Crew's top referral source. By September 30, 2013, Unsplash hit 1 million image downloads. By May 30, 2014, it had reached 10 million; by its second year, it had hit 30 million with worldwide reach; and by year three, it had topped 100 million downloads. Unsplash photos were used in ads for major brands like Pringles and featured in countless publications, including the front page of *The New York Times*.[25] In addition—Cho now had two successful companies.

Research is beginning to show that creativity is a skill that can be developed, much like any other.[26] Yes, some people seem more able to cultivate creativity than others, but being creative is also simply a matter of you seeing it, embracing it, and sharing it. According to Tucker Marion, associate professor at Northeastern University's D'Amore-McKim School of Business and director of the Masters of Science in Innovation program, "Creativity in business is a crucial first step that needs to be prioritized by senior leadership ... Creativity is what fuels big ideas, challenges employees' way of thinking, and opens the door to new business opportunities." Marion distinguishes, however, between creativity and innovation, stating that creativity is different; it's a mechanism to being innovative. You can have great ideas but not be innovative."[27]

A powerful point Marion makes is that creative leaders tend to be more comfortable with ambiguity. In order to realize any of our personal and collective potential, we must become more risk tolerant. Sometimes creative problem-solving can seem risky, but business is risky at its core! With the exception of you having to repay Uncle Sam and that bank loan, there are never any real guarantees.

I grew up in a home with a mother who was a painter and interior designer and a father who got creative in the yard and garden. Yet after years of working in our family business, I hadn't yet figured out how to put creativity together with the pragmatics of business—that was, until I began studying for my Executive MBA, when it became clear how creativity could be used. Cathy Anderson, our creativity-class teacher as well as a mystery writer and attorney (talk about using both sides of the brain), taught us how journaling and going on long "rambles" can give us fresh perspectives—to help our team and see more clearly (and spot much more than fires) from the fire tower. Most of us hadn't thought about the importance of creativity in business before that day and we walked out the door thinking differently about our own ability to be creative in business.

STEP BACK (TAKE A SELAH SECOND)

THE CATCH IN the creative process is that things can sometimes feel as though they have hit a dry spell. In these circumstances, curiosity helps to keep creativity flowing. When curiosity is maintained, it reopens (or keeps open) the continuity of creative thinking and problem-solving. It can also inspire both curiosity and creativity within others. Next time you reach a potential roadblock or new challenge, step back and think about which creative solutions could answer this question:

If we could do <u>anything</u> right now, what would we do?

STEP INTO ACTION

CREATIVITY IS SOMETHING you already know how to do (there's that good-news story coming into play again). It catches on when you overcome your fears and increase your belief in yourself and your team. Sometimes, all you need is a little extra time and space to discover it. When it comes to incorporating greater creativity in the daily grind of business, here are a few steps you can take:

1. **Think Critically about Creativity**

    As a leader, creative problem-solving can sound great in theory but not in execution, when you have deadlines looming for the things that creativity needs to be producing! Brainstorming needs to have boundaries to be effective and help you stay on track. Having a gateway to delve into creativity can help balance the worlds of business logic and creative conceptualization. Critical thinking, when applied to creativity, can help integrate creativity when you don't have the luxury of limitless time. Give yourself a sense of a hard stop, or at least the guardrails you need to create within. You might allow an hour in your schedule to go for a walk and be creatively thinking up potential solutions to a smaller problem, or else give yourself an entire quarter to create bigger-picture solutions. Whatever the process necessitates, have a sense of your time frame.

2. Find a Place Where You Feel Inspired

It can be challenging to be creative within a particular time frame. Making the most of "creating within the guardrails" means identifying the place and time when you feel inspired. What is that place where new ideas just seem to pop up? For some, it is in the simple everyday activities of going for a walk or taking a shower. For others, it happens during a long drive, while musing through a museum, or on a trip to a different country. For as many ways as you can be creative, there are just as many places and occasions where you can find greater creativity. Take the time to discover which ones work best for you, and go there often.

Creativity is not something you either have or don't. It is natural and a divinely derived element of being human that we can all tap into and has critical points of contact with the science of business). Creative potential lies in every one of us, and it comes from the place in our hearts that we fill with God. God is the ultimate creator, and we are all creative beings, because of the spirit God infuses us with. There is a beauty in understanding how wonderfully God has made us. Your gifts and talents are your contribution to society, and it is through creativity that you can express those gifts. All you need to do is allow time to be creative. Let yourself "go there" (to a creative space) and ask how you can make things better and just how great they can be. When you do, always be sure to come back to business, in order to integrate your innovative ideas, solutions, and visions every day, at the highest level you can possibly achieve.

CAPTURE YOUR FULL CREATIVE POTENTIAL

If you are not moving forward,
you are heading backward.

HAVE YOU EVER thought about what it would look like if you took a new job with another company? Have you pictured the intricate details of your dream home or dream vacation? If you have, you have used your creative powers to envision yourself in that ideal space. You have also harnessed the State of Being that aligns with capturing your full creative potential.

You know that person who does everything differently: They don't fit the norm and can be eclectic or esoteric and produce in a way that differs from what you've been taught. They might not always be the one talking, but they are most often the one laughing. People gravitate to them, even if it's slightly unsettling that they don't dance to the typical beat of the corporate drum; there's simply something about them that others like. They shine, even in those moments when they might question what the heck they are doing, and they do so because they have a deep, abiding centeredness that exudes a magnetic energy and quickly dispatches any doubts that arise in their minds. They have charisma, with depth and wisdom to back it up.

Sister Cintra Pemberton was one of those people for me. She was the author of *Soulfaring: Celtic Pilgrimages Then and Now* and a dedicated pilgrim. A student of pilgrimage history and an inspiration for those seeking new sites to visit, she had a way of moving others into heart-centered action, or as she would put it, the, "experience of the Holy in each place." When I first met Sister Cintra, she was carrying a paper bag and trying to discreetly deliver it to a friend who was sharing a row with me at church. I instantly loved both her energy and her puckish way of sneaking the bag under my friend's chair. When I asked her what was in the bag, she said, "Why, socks of course! I'm delivering festive socks to my friend who loves them." After church, I introduced myself to Cintra and quickly learned that she was in the Order of Saint Helena, a small order of nuns based out of Augusta, Georgia. The group's mission is "to show forth the love of Christ through a life of monastic prayer, hospitality, and service."[28] And boy, do they! Small but mighty, this order has led some of the greatest spiritual retreats and offered its pilgrims such exquisite examples of hospitality and graciousness as this pilgrim has ever seen. As our friendship blossomed, I witnessed Cintra in action as one of the group's operational leaders. She was well connected worldwide and kept a rigorous eye on expenditures, but not at the expense of the mission. She was a living example of the age-old adage to "spread the Gospel, and sometimes, use words." When she did use her words, they were true and kind—though they could be refreshingly sassy as well. Watching her made me realize that even if you have a challenging job, you can embrace it, do your best, be joyfully creative, and have so much fun, all at the same time. During the years our friendship grew, I came to experience Cintra as a creative and committed worker and leader, always quick with a laugh and a lesson. What she taught abides with me to this day. Her positive impact ran deep with those she touched.

Creative potential is the lifeblood of your organization; it is responsible for what is compelling to your internal and external customers, the bright flashing light that attracts people to your company, your products, and your services. It empowers you to create something that customers will become curious about—something they never thought they needed until you expressed something in such a manner that they were inspired to check you out, only to find you have something they undeniably want to be a part of. Capturing your full creative potential is about mining potential within yourself and your team members, and doing so in a way that contributes to forming a culture that is a bright shining light your external customers will see and feel.

STEP BACK (TAKE A SELAH SECOND)

IT IS OFTEN said that our greatest fear is fear of our own greatness. On this topic, global spiritual teacher

Marianne Williamson says, "We ask ourselves, 'Who am I to be brilliant, gorgeous, talented, fabulous?' Actually, who are you *not* to be?"[29] The thought *I'm not creative* is often tied to fear of failure. You worry that your ideas might be a bust or not as good as someone else's perceived "supreme creativity." Be aware, however, that the voice of fear and the voice of reason are two *very different voices,* and you must learn to be conscious of the fear voice (the shadow voice) in order to be able to then release it. Sit with the big creative ideas that you are currently holding in your heart, then ask yourself:

- *What positive potential am I afraid of unleashing?*

- *What could be possible if I "go there" and allow myself to create that potential?*

- *What type of freedom and free will would be unleashed?*

You can capture your full creative potential only when you release the weight of doubt and fear. This means addressing and eliminating fear from within yourself and then freeing the people in your organization from that same fear, should they be feeling it too. Carve out a noble space where you knock out the fear of reprisal and the golden calves. Because if you don't, you will be replicating the worst elements of your culture and sacrificing your creative potential.

STEP INTO ACTION

YOU CAN HAVE what brings you light and feels right for yourself and for your organization when you wholeheartedly *own your creative potential.* Take the steps necessary to branch out into newfound creative territory and take full ownership of the unique gifts you've been given in order to make the world and your organization a better place.

1. **Have Faith in the Creative Journey**

    Visualize your most positive outcome, because when creative solutions you have intentionally nurtured bear fruit, that in turn nourishes your employees, vendors, and clients, which is greatly fulfilling. Take more chances, which will eventually help build confidence and faith in yourself. Vet your ideas with a small, trusted group.

Having faith in the creative journey is a self-fulfilling prophecy. Creative potential isn't about some secret need to think of yourself as way out-there; creativity can develop effectively in the context of a business environment. Once you lift the veil from your eyes, see that you can be creative, and realize what has already resulted from your creative ideas, you can start to integrate more creativity in all your decisions. You can also allow yourself to enjoy the creative process and trust in the growth it will produce, regardless of whether you have wins or losses.

2. Let Yourself Grow

Capturing your full creative potential requires growth and the realization that there is no shame in change. Change is not only inevitable, it is the way of nature. Are you, say, still bound forever to the people you went to high school with? Are you even the same person you were back then? Chances are you've moved on from the young person you once were as you've matured and morphed into the adult you are now. Just as you can understand that time and experience change us, and that what worked for you then may no longer work for you now, you can also understand that growth never stops—not for you and not for your company. Do not shy away from allowing creativity to fuel change and growth for you and for your organization.

The exploration of your potential should always feel inclusive and encouraging. It should incorporate all the fruits of the Spirit: love, joy, peace, patience, kindness, goodness, gentleness, faithfulness, and self-control. These are the good things that you have the opportunity to mine within yourself on your journey of self-discovery and finding your drive—where you belong and are destined to share these gifts. The more faith you have in the creative journey, the more comfortable you become with who you are, and the more you can settle into the wisdom of knowing that failure is to be expected, the greater your chance of reaching the meadow of opportunity you seek.

We're not talking about something magical that you, your team, or your organization dream of; this is about energetically pulling yourself up to where you want to be, much like Sister Cintra Pemberton did, and then bringing into reality the solutions and ideas that will help you win more and lose less. Reaching your creative potential is going to be hard, thoughtful, heartful work. But it will be *you* who defines your potential and what you want. You will also realize your company's creative potential only by forming a culture that brings in the right people—others who believe in capturing their full creative potential. Give everyone the platform to be curious and share their creative gifts, and your results may become boundless. Then those bright, shiny lights that help others feel your mission will be right there for your external customers to see.

LEADING
WITH CARE

KNOW WHAT'S GOING ON BECAUSE YOU CARE

If your culture is less than ideal, it is going to blow everything else up.

WHEN THINGS GO downward at your organization, do you find yourself shocked or surprised? Or are you prepared and aware of the situation? At the same time, are you focused on treating people with kindness, empathy, and compassion?

While tuning into your curiosity and creative potential is necessary daily, it cannot come at the cost of critical matters requiring your attention. You can have the grandest visions for your individual and organizational potential, but without taking care to keep things on track, your visions will quickly derail. That said, it is human nature to want to avoid going into the weeds when you don't know what you'll find there, or even if you'll ever make it back out.

In her book *The Reflective Executive*, advertising executive Emilie Griffin, who has also done graduate work in theology, claims, "It is clear that the best entrepreneurial visions are founded in love."[30] Strategy won't fix itself, but having a great culture most definitely makes strategy creation easier and more enjoyable. Caring is the fuel that gets things going in the right way, driving implementation while protecting and celebrating your culture. You can't have a flourishing garden by tossing seeds down and never tending to it, or by not observing the weeds taking over. Your team is the same; they require constant connection. The health and longevity of your relationships with your internal and external clients are dependent on whether you are proactively acting out of care.

Knowing what's going on because you care is about knowing and being in tune with the pulse of your departments and people. It is about connecting with yourself and with others on a deeply human level. It is also about compassion, kindness, empathy, and love as you include and empower the right people at the right time. It starts with the decision to be an excellent company and to treat people with love and respect. This includes your employees, your customers, your vendors, your neighbors, and your community. Seeing and acting on all things through a lens of care will guide you to do the right thing, because you are being thoughtful about what you are doing, and that is what creates a good culture.

When I first joined Vistage in 2015, I was fresh out of graduate school and new to being CEO, and I just wanted to do the right thing. Leadership development teacher and former Vistage chair Chalmers Brothers was one of our first speakers. During his talk, he repeated the words attributed to management consultant Peter Drucker: "Culture eats strategy for breakfast." Essentially, no management strategy, no matter how strong, will endure if you don't have a culture of people ready to implement and grow it.[31] Those words cut through and created a watershed moment for me, as I recognized the need to flip my focus to caring about culture in a whole new way. Strategy had been at the forefront of my mind, yet I could now see that if our culture was less than ideal, even the best of strategies could not enhance it.

If you aren't getting the people you want into your organization, those who exhibit the level of capacity and care you need, check your bait. Would your job postings make you want to work at your company? Are they reflective of your culture, and is that culture what you want it to be? Time spent enhancing your culture and getting it back on track will always be the best use of your time. Plans and processes can be replicated, but you can't duplicate discipline and love—love for each other and for the experience your customers and employees are having. Take the time to dig a little deeper with a high level of care for those you serve. Hire those who are willing to do the same. That way, you can create your culture intentionally and shape your strategies around what will best support that culture.

STEP BACK (TAKE A SELAH SECOND)

RELATIONAL MANAGEMENT AND strengthening your culture through care start with awareness of how you act when alone and in close relationships. Only then can you assess what your relationships look like at work. It is important for each and every one of us to have people in our lives cheering us on, telling us that they know who we are and encouraging us with their confidence that we are going to crush it. In order to help you become that person for others, take a moment to ask yourself:

- *Who are the people showing me the greatest level of care?*

- *What can I learn from them and apply to how I care for others?*

STEP INTO ACTION

Loving work doesn't have to be in health care or retirement homes only. It can be found in for-profit, capitalistic business. Being a corporate CEO means you are operating a mission-based field, and that creating a culture of care is everybody's responsibility. The CEO sets the standards, but everyone has to live, breathe, and demonstrate them daily. If you have a crappy culture, not even the best-intended strategies will stick. Here are some steps you can take to ensure you are in tune with the humanity of your organization at all times:

1. **Check the Metrics**

   You find out what's going on in your company by looking at the metrics (the score of what's going on with the people therein). If you are off with a metric, you then have to decide if it is a one-off or a systemic issue. If it is systemic, is it a people problem, a process problem, or both? Most issues can be fixed, though when things have fallen fully off the rails, sometimes people and processes need to be changed. (More on having those tough conversations in the next chapter.) Make the necessary changes. Maybe you will get it right the next time, and maybe you won't. You just have to keep at it.

2. **Maintain Mindfulness**

   Responsibility and accountability are effective as long as you are able to act with compassion for those who are being held to these standards. In your every word and action, think about its potential impact on those you lead. Humanize things, and communicate with the intention of truly understanding where others are coming from. Allow yourself to care about the experiences they are having and how they might receive things, while still holding them accountable and responsible for their own actions.

3. **Set Boundaries**

Caring means talking to the stakeholders involved, then making the decisions that will help improve your culture. Sometimes that will also involve knowing whether to personally take accountability and action, or whether the situation merits coaching a team to make a decision (and hopefully finding their own potential in the process).

When it comes to caring, boundaries are extremely important. Your direct reports can obviously help you understand what may be happening with their team, yet it's up to you to lead them in managing whatever issues arise and not putting their work back on you; the trick is knowing when "the monkeys" (or the entire circus) are not yours to take on. While you want to show empathy and compassion, you also don't want to risk becoming emotionally overwhelmed. You can't see the lay of the land from the fire tower if you're down in the bush putting out fires. Boundaries will help ensure that you can maintain a high level of care for yourself and for others while having the eyes to see the bigger picture.

As a leader, your power lies in holding yourself and others accountable with a high level of care for the human component of business. No one will let you get away with saying you don't know or don't remember what is going on within your company. CEOs get interviewed on CNBC and called to Congress because it is expected that they know what is going on in their company and are responsible for it. When you operate from a standpoint of authenticity, caring becomes something you naturally want to do. The love and compassion you give to others will become a gift people can use for the rest of their lives. It is arguably more important than any other skill set, because executing anything without care will likely only lead to things crumbling.

HAVE THE TOUGH
CONVERSATIONS

If you want a great culture, you have to be
willing to have the tough conversations.

WHEN FACED WITH having to approach a team member about a difficult situation, do you feel equipped or are you emotionally exhausted before you even get started? How do you step into having to part ways with one of your team members?

If you want a healthy company with a great culture, you must be willing to navigate the messy maneuvers and have the tough conversations required to get there. The hard truth is that the ability to have these tough conversations is what makes the difference between a good CEO and a great CEO. Showing up for others is critical, but sweeping things under the rug will only lead to quickly running out of rugs—or brooms big enough to handle the mess. In order to build the right culture, you need to take things one mess at a time and have the tough conversations the right way. If you are leading people, you likely understand what it means to have hard conversations. Sometimes you may have to separate with someone because their role or employment with you is just not working out. Sometimes you may be tasked with putting the wheels back on a car as it is hurtling down the freeway.

Susan Scott, founder and CEO of global leadership development and training company Fierce, Inc., and author of the national bestseller *Fierce Conversations*, has spent the past two decades working to encourage companies to have conversations that tie directly to the bottom line while also enriching relationships. In her talk "Why Fierce," she says:

> *What gets talked about in a company and how it gets talked about and who gets invited to the conversation determines what is going to happen and what is not going to happen ... While we are developing products and services, we are*

nurturing (or not nurturing) human be-
ings. We understand the financial and
human costs of conversations and meet-
ings that are pointless. I think that point-
less conversations are really the source
of many of our struggles. You solve that
issue and you solve your struggles.[32]

We've all had at least one challenging leader who was inordinately hard on us, or even abusive. Chances are that in those circumstances you've learned a hard lesson about standing up for yourself and telling that person how their words or behavior made you feel. None of us wants to be our own old tough boss, because we know that negativity can be a force multiplier to the same degree as positivity. How you show up in the toughest, most fiery moments should be the same way you show up in the moments that require the greatest sensitivity and care.

Taking on the hard conversations is something you do in service to others. As human beings, we must all have them, though we want to have them in the best, most productive and supportive way possible. Most of us have them with our spouse or partner, with family members, or with close friends. As CEO, the number of relationships and tough conversations you need to manage is multiplied exponentially. There is a lot being asked of you from a relational management standpoint, but it is still possible to bring the same level of care to your work relationships as you do to your personal ones.

STEP BACK (TAKE A SELAH SECOND)

WHEN YOU OPERATE earnestly and honestly from a basis of love, it maximizes the chances of success with the "care-frontational" or more difficult conversations that need to be had. Still, you have to be mentally and emotionally equipped for the questions and topics coming your way. Taking a breath is where it all starts. Before your next tough conversation, stop and ask yourself:

Where is my breath?

Breathe deeply. Then ask,

What is my present State of Being? Am I anxious? Why? Am I angry? Why?

Lovingly and gently take yourself through the exploration of *why*. Then hit Reset as you remind yourself that you are centered and have within yourself all that's necessary for what you need to do.

STEP INTO ACTION

CREATING A GREAT culture and implementing the strategy to create ideal results means that every day you must discern where the hard conversations are that you need to be having, and then go have them. Here are some tips to ensure you have what it takes to fulfill this work:

1. **Think about the Other Person**

    Even during the hardest of conversations, you can act out of love. Think about the other person—their needs, their concerns, their emotions. Be honest and direct, while showing care and compassion. By being an empathy-driven leader, you bring your best possible State of Being to the table. It requires self-work to not come at another person when the situation is sticky or you are feeling irritated. Thinking about their perspective always allows for greater empathy. When you start using the tool of empathy in your conversations, you also get more feedback, both verbal and nonverbal. Need a practice run? Talk to an empty chair and envision the conversation unfolding.

2. Address What Needs to Be Addressed

When you are willing to address what needs to be addressed with your team, you are able to start fixing issues. Two important points to remember along the way, though: (1) Be authentic about the deficiencies within yourself that should be addressed to elevate your leadership and ensure you go into the tough conversations in your best State of Being; (2) Don't rush it; tough conversations don't need to be happening every moment of every day. Sometimes it's best to give things some grace and space to work themselves out a bit.

3. Keep Refilling Your Empathy Well

Overextending yourself mentally and emotionally can make you feel incapable of taking on what is yet to come your way. It is okay to feel pain for others, because that means you have awareness. It is also okay to ask for insight, support, and help in turning things around, for yourself and your organization. If you skip the moments to refill your own emotional well and go back to doing the day-to-day, things will likely start to unravel, and situations will look uglier. When you feel your empathy waning, pause from looking at the people or processes that might be causing you stress and look at what you are doing for yourself. In order to go into the world with empathy and care every day, you need to take care of yourself. Emotional recharging can be achieved through many of the refueling exercises discussed earlier, such as walking in nature or morning meditation.

4. Let Hiring Be an Opportunity

If you reach a point where you have determined the need to replace a team member, open your eyes to finding a super person to fill that position. Simultaneously use this as an opportunity to reexamine the dynamics of the department and how it is set up, and hire someone who can make your organization better, faster, and stronger.

Care must always come first. It is something that you are either doing or not; there is no middle ground. Some might claim that you can't have care and love in business, but the fact is you absolutely can; you just need to find it within yourself and offer it to others. Being a leader or CEO is not an easy job, but when you enter into conversations at a deeply human and caring level, magic starts to happen. It's hard work, and you won't always get a thank you, but you'll know when things feel right. Have faith in yourself and the belief that you have what it takes to handle any situation that is in front of you. You can overcome hurdles by looking back at how you solved similar problems or failures in the past. Let the positive parallels move you forward with greater ease, and let the differences provide learning opportunities to do things better next time around.

A great culture won't create itself, just as the tough conversations won't happen by themselves. When it comes to those difficult times, you can delegate the work, but you can't delegate ultimate responsibility.

Regardless of whether you are fueling your ultimate potential or putting out fires to get back on track, you must *want to* go bravely into it, addressing things and being willing to clean them up. The more willing you are to step up and prioritize having the hard talks, the more continuously you will create a healthy culture throughout your entire organization—the day-to-day happenings of the living, breathing organism. Make the decision that you want to be the type of leader who operates with empathy and love, and you will be offered opportunities to show up that way more and more often.

MAKE THE MOST IMPORTANT THING THE MOST IMPORTANT THING

Your mission and values are not just there to impress; they should move you into action.

WHEN YOU ARE in the thick of a challenge or crisis, how do you decide the best course of action?? How do you qualify your decision? How do you decide what will lead to the best result for your internal and external customers?

Often in business you will find yourself in uncharted territory, navigating terrain for which you don't have a map. But when you have a mission and clarity on your most important things—the guiding principles that represent what your organization stands for—you are never truly without a map. Allow your mission and principles to guide you, and you will always have something bigger leading you. Making the most important thing the most important thing is about always having the purposeful bigger picture top of mind and allowing it to guide decisions. It's also about having the discipline to really sit with something and make it a priority, based on alignment with your guiding principles. If you allow other forces to sway your plans, you may end up unnecessarily shuffling people around, letting people go, changing salaries, upending processes, and reworking whole departments. And you don't need those added tasks on your plate.

Adventure outfitter Patagonia has always marched to its own beat. Since Yvon Chouinard started the Earth-friendly clothing company with a few friends in 1973, Patagonia has done things its own way, never collaborating with a fashion brand or influencers or promoting their products in fashion magazines.[33] They have chosen to make the planet their priority, pledging 1% of all sales to the preservation and restoration of the natural environment since 1985. Over the years, they have awarded more than $140 million to grassroots environmental groups having a positive impact in local communities, and they pride themselves on collaborating with and sharing the stories of these people.[34] Why? Because they are in business to save the planet.[35] This mission is clearly depicted through the company's decisions, collaborations, and communication. Yet founder Yvon Chouinard did not consider this enough. Protecting the planet and supporting others doing it was so critical that in 2018, Patagonia redefined their mission statement to "Patagonia is in business to save our home planet."[36] This new, even further clarified mission was supported by previously established core values:

1. *Build the best product.*
2. *Cause no unnecessary harm.*
3. *Use business to protect nature.*
4. *Not bound by convention.*[37]

In an interview with *Vogue* magazine, forty-eight-year veteran Patagonia employee Vincent Stanley shared how the company's environmental mission flows throughout the organization: "What we really focus on is quality: What constitutes quality at Patagonia? How do we have a shared definition? And the second is environmentalism: How is it important to people in the different roles in the company?"[38] Patagonia proves the points that putting your mission first does ultimately direct you to take care of others in an all-encompassing way, and that your core values are something that you should be living every day. Your vision then becomes your ability to look at everything through the lens of your mission and values. It becomes the filter that helps you always make the most important thing the most important thing.

While most missions become "statements," they should ultimately be seen as the bigger picture and North Star that guides everything. Most business schools teach the importance of creating a mission, a vision, and core values for an organization. Yet so often, companies do so in a capacity whereby hours, days, and dollars are spent crafting powerful verbiage that does nothing more than sit in a framed plaque in the corporate entranceway or the ivory tower. Without living and breathing the mission and values every day and prioritizing the people in your organization, creating a mission is all a waste of time. Your mission, values, and any associated language are not just there to impress; they should be both aspirational and realistic. They should move you into action.

STEP BACK (TAKE A SELAH SECOND)

EVERY ONE OF us has past habits and limited attention spans at certain times, but when you send good out into the world, more good starts to happen. Every day, you can ask yourself:

> *How can I help others pull together to support our company mission on a daily basis?*

STEP INTO ACTION

IF YOU HAVE become a CEO or leader, you already have what it takes to realize the behaviors required to be a great leader. Now it is time to get excited about being your best self and helping others become their best selves. Here are some steps to ensure that the most important thing remains the most important thing, and that you are always moving forward in alignment with your mission, people, and potential:

1. Look at How You Are Treating Your Team

Your values are the lens through which you need to make every decision, including how you treat others. Take the time to step back and assess whether you are leading with empathy, having the tough conversations where they need to be had, and inspiring your team to move forward in alignment with your mission and values. Appreciate all that those in your organization have accomplished and all that you have accomplished. You want to be the mirror you hope to see, reflecting a better way.

2. Look at How You Are Treating Yourself

Your personal ethos—what you stand for, what you stand against, what you want to give, and what you will not tolerate—is what builds true character. Check in with yourself to see where you are from a humanity standpoint. Recheck your State of Being before making any decisions or having any sensitive conversations. Does it align with what your company wants to stand for? You have to hold yourself accountable for sustaining company values in order to get everyone else to do it too.

3. Measure against the Mission

To determine what needs to be done as a priority, ask whether that need or project aligns with your core values and mission. Rank the needs to determine whether they are the most important thing and whether they should rise up the priority scale. Do they align with your core values? Is the action required immediate? Remember to make the people involved the most important criteria for every decision. What do they need? Are they in danger or crisis? How is what is happening affecting all the people involved? When you find yourself in challenging situations where you feel you don't know what to do, three simple questions, which parallel the three important actions above, can help guide you. Ask your team the following:

- *Are you okay?*

- *Are we okay?*

- *Are we still in line with our mission?*

Let your company be different and stand for something different. Making people and your mission the most important things means always being attentive and willing to step in, assess, support, and pivot as required. If the answers to these questions are not affirmative, take action to realign with what is most important. Once the answers are yes, you can continue forging forward. It should always be about the mission and the people involved. True, there's no denying that most missions come back to money, in one form or another. Profit is important, and none of us should ever apologize for that, because without it you go out of business and are no longer around to take care of your internal and external customers. But prioritizing people does not have to mean neglecting profit. Measure all decisions against the mission and know that when you make it about your internal and external customers, the money will come.

DOGGED
DETERMINATION

BECOME BETTER, FASTER, STRONGER TOGETHER

*Just because you know the answer
doesn't mean you always have to
be the one to come up with it.*

THERE IS SOMETHING that needs to get done or be decided within your organization. You know how to get the team there, but will you tell them? Does your taking on the problem-solving mean you are taking something away from them?

When time is of the essence, when you are embroiled in a crisis and you have supported your team but they aren't able to come up with the answer, you may inevitably have to "tell" rather than "sell." In most cases, however, just because you know the answers to a question or solutions to a problem doesn't mean you always have to be the one to come up with them. You can build your team with the right folks for the right jobs—proactive, disciplined people who want to be entrusted to do the work. You can teach them their jobs (science) and let them operate using their gifts, talents, and heart (art). You can give them the tools, resources, one-to-ones, kudos, and coaching they need—but then you must *let them do their work!*

In 2007, the latest CEO of Popeyes Louisiana Kitchen, Inc. had just resigned, bringing the total CEOs the company had been through to four in seven years. The company was struggling from a lack of strategy and an overabundance of short-term thinking. There was little new product innovation, no national advertising (or subsequently cemented consumer awareness), and no brand-building ideas. Sales were a choppy reflection of a lack of internal consistency, and everything had snowballed into angry and frustrated franchisees. Cheryl Bachelder, who had served as a senior executive with two other fast-food giants, was asked to join the board search committee to hire a new CEO. When two candidates turned down the job, the board invited her to step into the role. Her monumental task, alongside her team, was to "both regain the franchisees' trust and fire up their enthusiasm for the future." [39]

In a humbling encounter with a franchise owner who spoke openly about the mistreatment they had received in the past, Bachelder realized that until the Popeyes leadership demonstrated value to their owners, they could not expect those owners to show enthusiasm for the future or be a part of any kind of turnaround. After questioning what kind of leaders they wanted to be and regaining sight of the fact that the franchisees were those with the most skin in the game within the organization, Bachelder and her team chose to focus intently on the franchisees, rather than on other stakeholders. They wanted to measure their success by franchisees' success, and they would do so through the practice of servant leadership. After gathering input from franchise owners, the Popeyes leadership team outlined a plan to initiate national advertising. To do so, they sacrificed short-term earnings in the name of gaining systemwide franchise alignment. They pushed through the 2008 recession and focused on new product innovation, and their market share grew from the teens to the mid-twenties. By 2016, one third of the Popeyes locations had been built within the previous five years, and the intention was to open an additional 200 or more global locations a year. The one lagging indicator was franchisee trust, and Bachelder continued to maintain open lines of communication with the franchisees. "It feels unfair sometimes," she said, referring to sacrificing short-term earnings for the sake of gaining trust and alignment, "but it's our job to keep modeling and earning trust."[40]

As a leader, when you have chosen to put others first, it creates ownership and allows you to tap into the genius of the group and get their insights on the process. They are in the trenches, and they need to be influencing the process. Let them be the ones to fix things! Let them take their tool bag of things they've been working on and solve the problem. This philosophy is a win-win; it leaves your employees feeling trusted, connected, and appreciated by using their insights to lead the company to success. Instead of coming into a challenge with guns blazing and saying, "This is the way we've always done it," or, "I'm going to do it," try instead asking, "This is the process we have now. How can we improve upon it?" The people of your organization will thus be forging the stable infrastructure of your company, and in the process, they will become great trainers themselves, as they pass on empowerment to others.

Instead of taking either the win for solving the problems or the tedious details of everyone's to-do lists, take on the greater role of coach, advisor, and consultant. Empowerment means not only learning how to value your team members' independence and boundaries, but also being their champion. As a leader, you are there to teach others about themselves, while giving them the tools and resources they can use to execute their role. To do so, you have to know how to work with others appropriately to empower them. Of course, you can always hold the answer in your mind, in case your team needs you to sprinkle in any seeds of insight. These are the actions of a leader who knows the value of empowerment and that they don't have to have all the answers, despite stereotypes of what you should be or do as a leader.

Where you are exercising authentic free will, there must also be strategic restraint, which involves a determination and commitment to empowering others. This position is harder to execute than simply telling someone how to solve a problem, because there has to be a paradigm shift within you as a leader—a shift that involves understanding that the more noble work is leading people into their best selves while giving them permission to stand in their power.

In the 2018 *Harvard Business Review* article "When Empowering Employees Works, and When It Doesn't," authors Allan Lee, Sara Willis, and Amy Wei Tian share insights from their work examining 105 empowerment studies, with data from more than 30,000 employees in thirty countries. They looked at whether an empowering leadership style was linked to improved job performance. Their findings, published in the *Journal of Organizational Behavior*, were telling:

1. Empowering leaders are much more effective at influencing employee creativity and citizenship behavior (i.e., behavior that is not formally recognized or rewarded, like helping coworkers or attending work functions that aren't mandatory) than routine task performance.

2. By empowering their employees, these leaders are also more likely to be trusted by their subordinates, compared with leaders who do not empower their employees.[41]

Your team wants to know that they are not alone and that you are right there behind them, without reaching over from the back seat and taking hold of the steering wheel. Remember that the purest definition of "it's on you" means accepting the role and responsibility of helping those you serve understand that they have potential; that they have everything they need within to realize that potential; and that they can be better, faster, and stronger than they ever imagined.

STEP BACK (TAKE A SELAH SECOND)

BECOMING BETTER, FASTER, and stronger together is about being able to look at your role as CEO through a different lens and understand the greater role therein: being a champion for your team. The ultimate goal should always be to have your team members willingly go and try things. You want them to come back to you and let you know if the idea worked or didn't work, and then tell you why. The next question then becomes, What do you want to do now? (Just as it was in regard to your own personal corporate journey.) Take a moment to ponder where you currently are on the paradigm shift toward becoming an empowering leader. Ask yourself the following question daily:

Am I giving my people the opportunity to be their best selves and step into their power?

STEP INTO ACTION

INSPIRE AND INSTRUCT without interfering—that is the name of the empowerment game. You can build the teams within your organization to function independently and appreciate the freedom that underpins healthy interdependence. Here are some powerful pointers:

1. Shape a Balanced Self-View

If you have an overly inflated view of yourself, it is unlikely that you will treat yourself or others right. The same holds true for an undervaluing yourself or underappreciating your team. You can find a healthy middle ground by taking the time to always be aware of your State of Being and the state of your personal growth. All that your team can be starts with you.

2. Make Conversations Out of Questions

Regularly check in with your team to see what the organization is doing that no longer needs to be done ... or what you aren't doing that should be done! These conversations should always end with a question mark, not a period or an exclamation point. Coaching and empowerment are about selling an idea or question so that the other person can do the thinking and arrive at the answer themselves. When you start a conversation with a direct report, consider setting your phone timer for three minutes. Be sure not to talk more than the allotted time. Give yourself space to ask questions and truly *listen* to their answers.

You can also build "buffer time" into your schedule and your meetings to help prioritize the most important things and give yourself and others room to breathe. When there are so many things to discuss, it can become all too easy to blow up the agenda. It is much more rewarding to allow time for your team to talk and to allow concepts start to evolving. Most times in the process, this will allow them to solve their own problems.

3. **Shift Your Focus to Fun**

   Empowering others might also mean shifting your views on what is fun. Leading your team with lightness in your coaching questions is important, as you witness them answer and make the right decisions on their own. Celebrate them, and they will generate a confident State of Being.

Every interaction and conversation can become an opportunity for empowerment when you allow it to. Give others the opportunity to decide what to do, and let them go do it! Every teacher is not a CEO, but every CEO is a teacher. The long-haul positive impact of leading with empowerment means knowing how best to tell your teams and people, *You can do this!* Give them a gift they will love: being able to take ownership. Make them contributors on the continuum of building the organization. Ultimately, even while you are working the answers out in your mind, you want to give those you serve the love, support, and freedom to exercise *their* free will. Also, remember never to give a support without challenging others to grow by setting a new goal to be achieved. This way, you will always push their determination and potential.

IF THE OX IS IN THE DITCH, DO WHAT IS NECESSARY TO GET IT OUT

If you walk past a mistake today, there is no way you are getting past what gets stuck in the crevice of that mistake tomorrow.

WHAT HAPPENS WHEN those larger-than-life problems hit you at 10:00 a.m. on a Tuesday morning or 4:00 p.m. on a Friday afternoon, and you're left feeling like nothing can move forward until they are fixed?

Something I was taught by my family was that when the ox was in the ditch, you had to do what was necessary to get it out, even on a Sunday! Back in the day, oxen were used to plow fields, and on occasion while working the fields, they would slip into the ditch. In order to finish plowing the fields, as well as ensure the animal was safe, the farmer would have to stop everything and get the ox out. In the corporate context, that ox could be an imminent threat or something significant impeding your ability to move forward or do business. It interrupts the flow, halts your processes, and sets you off course. It might be a software rollout gone bad, where you are sold a certain expectation and end up with a host of conversion issues instead. It may an employee, vendor, or client with a steadfast dedication to hijacking your mission. Regardless of what shape it takes, it represents an urgent situation and an obstacle obstructing your view of all that lies beyond it. It is also something that can quickly become widespread if not tended to immediately, because part of your job is to see the threats that are coming and do everything in your power to avoid those bigger-than-business problems bottlenecking your every next move.

As a leader, your typical role is to provide resources for others to solve problems. You measure results and coach the *process*. But during these times of imminent threat, you just have to step in. When it comes to "ox extractions," it's time for you to be less of a coach and more of a director and the voice of the company, making the immediate tough calls that will move things forward. Like a coach calling an unexpected time-out to make an urgent change in play, you must be willing to get in there and do what is necessary.

For years, I lived with a fire in my heart that I knew went beyond the standard determination or grit many of us are familiar with. I didn't have a name for that little something extra that allows us to push beyond previous limits in times of crisis—not until I encountered the work of Elisabet Lahti, PhD. It was then that I realized that this "something" had a name. Lahti, the contributor of this book's foreword, is a global expert on the Finnish term *sisu*, which she defines as "extraordinary perseverance and intestinal fortitude that can help the individual push through even the most unbearable challenges and go beyond one's *assumed* mental or physical capacities."[42] She affirms that:

> *Strength to find acceptance and contentment in a moment when facing insurmountable headwind (or even ceasing*

from further action if this leads to more
beneficial long-term outcomes) is devel-
oped through the 'humanly tuned effort'
of systems intelligence that can bring ex-
cellence into even our extraordinary feats
by rendering our inner strength more
life-giving to the system as a whole.[43]

This inner fortitude that all of us possess in those moments of facing seemingly larger-than-life (or business) obstacles requires ongoing awareness—of ourselves, our people, and our progress as an organization. It is also rooted in a healthy dose of extraordinary perseverance, which Lahti dubs "an experience of 'becoming-into-being'[44] in which that which becomes-to-be is an expanded experience of our capacities in a point where the realities of 'giving up' and 'going on' both linger a mere breath away." In Martha Brown terms, that means your State of Being has shifted and evolved to the point of awakening new ability.

STEP BACK (TAKE A SELAH SECOND)

SOME DECISIONS SIMPLY need to be made by the CEO alone, and in those cases, the buck stops with the CEO. If you have messes you need to clean up, you clean them up. If you need to adapt and adjust, you do that too. There's a tendency to hide behind what you don't know or what you think you don't know. When imminent threats appear, it is going to force a huge cleanup, and that's when it's best to be proactive. Rally your team and think about what your next change or rollout is really going to look like. Then ask yourself:

- *What do the warning signs of potential threats look like?*

- *If things don't go the way we think they will go, how will we handle it?*

STEP INTO ACTION

WHEN I WAS growing up, my mother's cousin was in the forestry service. I remember them coming through and cutting "fire breaks" to limit the spread of potential fires. When you've proactively established such "fire breaks" in the form of taking care to clean up messes and mistakes as you go, you can lessen the impact and devastation of big threats. That's just mitigating risk. Here are some steps you can take to get the ox out of the ditch (if it is already in there) or become proactively present to potential threats in the first place:

1. Don't Walk Past a Mistake

Hard decision = easy life. Easy decision = hard life. There will always be a cost to walking past a mistake. Either you pay a little now, or you pay a lot later. If you wait, the problems become much more complex and typically involve multiple people. If you are aware of a way to make things better, do it. Take ownership and make your motto, *If you see something, say something—or ask something!* If you don't ask more questions and work to fully understand and solve the issue(s) at hand, you are walking past a mistake.

2. Hold People Accountable

It's on you. You don't have to know everything, but you do have to accept accountability. If you want a great culture, you need to ask yourself how you are willing to grow. Hold yourself accountable and teach your company the same thing. Have your team members go back and fix their mistakes. It will save things from escalating to the point of catastrophe.

In addition, the best proactive measure you can take is to ask, *What will the recourse be if X happens?* You also have to have some idea of the answers to just about everything, even the big threats.

3. Have No Golden Calves

Golden calves are goals you are unwilling to release, but they can also be people. ("We'll let Sally get away with not following protocol because she sells a lot.") Sometimes you have to drop or adjust a goal, and other times you have to be willing to question the status quo. In seeking a new solution, you may actually discover a problem you didn't even know existed. If you ideate the "what ifs" and plan for pitfalls before they occur, you can quickly address them before/when they do and avoid having a catastrophe on your hands. As for the Sallys, they can't be allowed to get away with breaking the procedures, because (1) it's not fair to everyone else following the rules, and (2) if you think Sally can continue side-stepping your processes and still be successful in the long term (along with your company), you are merely fooling yourself. If you believe in your processes and procedures, teach others why. At the same time, loosen your grip on your golden calves and open yourself to discovery, because that calf may actually be an ox in disguise.

Following the devastating three-million-acre fires across Idaho and Montana in August 1910, the United States Forest Service (USFS) began building lookout towers in national forests to aid in fire detection across the country. In 1911, USFS forester William Bushnell Osborne, Jr., invented the "firefinder" for use in the lookouts, a rotating steel disk designed to accurately point out the location of fires by sighting smoke in the distance.[45] You've heard me reference the fire tower throughout this book, and here is its main application. Once you have resolved the imminent threat you then have to get back up in the fire tower and continue overseeing the business. As a leader, you must have the eyes to see the fires or groundswells—in all shapes and sizes—that can come rushing in and take over. The caveat is that all of this, even with the best instrumentation in the modern world at your fingertips, will not work unless you have the gusto and willingness to keep going back up into your metaphorical fire tower. And that is a process that requires true determination and *sisu*.

If you end up with an ox blocking your progress, you must be willing to drop everything, reallocate resources, meet with the right people, and have the right conversations. Time is of the essence. Getting past that obstacle will be messy and uncomfortable and may change your schedule, at least for a little while, but you have to do what it takes to triage these big events to quickly get back on track. And you do it because once cleared, those sometimes catastrophic and almost always challenging obstacles may actually reveal a new way forward.

TAKE TIME TO REFUEL

There is a time limit to even a
seemingly limitless work ethic.

DO YOU HAVE the desired energy and appetite to take on your every day? Do you feel how you need to feel in order to create what you want to be, do, and have?

When it comes to the dogged pursuit of business objectives, the grind is real, and resilience, courage, grit, faith, and fuel are key. But what happens when you have exhausted every possible personal source from both ends? If you are constantly pushing forward, carrying the weight of current burdens, chances are you will eventually run out of steam, or at the very least start making really bad decisions. As a population, we act as if workaholism—a term defined not solely by the moments we're working but also the moments when we're thinking about the work we should be doing—is simply what's necessary to be a productive and impactful leader, but the truth is, there is always a limit to even an apparently limitless work ethic. Without time to refresh, you aren't ever going to do your job well. If you're burnt out, your work will suffer, as will your team and those goals you had set your sights on. Things will inevitably hit a tipping point where you become unproductive, as busyness and burnout intersect and cause unhealthiness.

In their paper "Grit: Sustained Self-Regulation in the Service of Superordinate Goals," psychologists Lauren Eskreis-Winkler, James J. Gross, and Angela L. Duckworth found that "research on self-regulation has illuminated the importance of aligning actions with intentions in order to achieve one's objectives. Research on grit adds an appreciation for the extreme stamina with which singular objectives are pursued over time. It likewise adds an appreciation for the steadfast effort that enables extraordinary accomplishment."[46] But there's a caveat to what these psychologists term grit, or the "dogged pursuit of a singular goal over years, over-coming obstacles, setbacks, failures, and all else that stands in the way."[47] That caveat is that the "steadfast effort" it requires is unrealistic without time to refuel. Workaholism is an old, outdated trope. No one is de-signed to work effectively or continuously from Monday to Friday, 9:00 to 5:00 (or longer, if you are CEO). You can't be a superhero every minute of every day, because it's hard to keep moving forward with dogged deter-mination when the armor you've been wearing starts weighing you down and your jetpack has run out of fuel.

I didn't give myself permission to take a break until I was well into my role as CEO, when exhaustion and burnout had begun to creep in. After joining Vistage, I discovered that my fellow CEOs were also not taking required vacation time. Our chair (and my coach), Kurt Graves, impressed upon us the importance of taking time away to reset. It was a strategy that was echoed in my Executive MBA education at Queens. I have always been in tune with when I needed to just step away from the office and go sit on the grass, but I didn't always empower myself to do it. Other voices in my head often told me it was ridiculous to need to do it. But once I learned to step away and take a real personal retreat (for longer than fifteen minutes out of the weeds), I would come back exponentially happier, more peaceful, and more productive. The one-to-one conversations I had with my team became even more productive than before, further fueling the engine of determination. And shockingly, my leaders didn't collapse and the company didn't blow up because I'd gone away!

The Covid pandemic pushed us to demand greater flexibility and shone a spotlight on the importance of having a State of Well-Being. Nothing is more important than your health and how you manage that at work. You can't expect a car to run forever without taking time to refuel. (Yes, electric vehicle owners, this applies to you too.) Taking time to refuel is about giving yourself permission to take care of yourself in the way that only you know you need to be cared for. Choose to no longer follow those outdated or expected behaviors that may result in your being stressed beyond the point of good health. Rejuvenate by going out into the world and doing something that refuels your heart, soul, and mind.

STEP BACK (TAKE A SELAH GETAWAY)

THE IMPORTANCE OF "retreating" cannot be overstated. This doesn't mean running away at the sight of that ox in the ditch or from a dauntingly hard conversation, jam-packing the family car, and heading for your favorite getaway. Retreating means going away on a solo mission, where you can go into the silence of your "inner thicket" and take time to just *be*. It is about being somewhere where you can hear yourself think (or not think) and where you get solutions without the strain of overthinking. Envision, meditate, pray (connecting to whatever source or higher power you believe in), exercise, exhale. You don't always need to come to a full halt; sometimes a retreat can be just a pit stop along the journey. Ask yourself:

- *Where can I go to refuel?*

- *What can I do that will leave me feeling truly recharged?*

- *What does it look like when I take this time for myself?*

- *What is the impact on my team?*

STEP INTO ACTION (OR NON-ACTION)

RETREATING IS A process you must train yourself to get used to. There are easy steps you can take to course-correct in the direction of refueling, and living in your authenticity is always the best directive. In the words of Brené Brown, "True belonging doesn't require you to change who you are, it requires you to be who you are."[48] When it comes to building your determination muscles and prioritizing retreats, try to keep these pointers in mind:

1. **Know and Honor What You Want**

   When it comes to refueling, you can get advice and you can educate yourself, but ultimately, you need to try things to know what works for you. Check in with yourself. Refueling is a two-way street: when you find the kind of retreat you need and give it to yourself, you will be able to tune into your vision for yourself, for your organization, and for your overall success. Honor the realizations that come your way as you find your best method of refueling.

2. Trust Yourself

Gaining awareness of when you need to refuel and how best you can do this comes from being honest with yourself about what you are seeing, feeling, and sensing all of the time. Communication with your body, your spirit, and your energy is paramount if you're going to know where you are on the burnout meter. Every human being—from performers to athletes to professionals—comes equipped with this sense. Knowing what you want and making choices in alignment with your authenticity boils down to trusting yourself. Maybe you have rituals you want to honor. If you work best in the morning and need a little break in the afternoon, build your schedule around that. Give yourself permission to go on the journey to figure out how you tick and when you do your best work. Then change gears when needed. And be sure to set healthy boundaries so you and your team honor your refueling time.

3. Build in "Buffer Time"

Many great leaders support the idea of buffer time, or building free time into your schedule to proactively prepare for the unexpected and to give yourself required breathing room to reset or discover new inspiration. Former LinkedIn CEO Jeff Weiner is one of those leaders. In a 2018 CNBC interview, he shared the concept of leaving ninety minutes of buffer time in your schedule every day.[49] It was a principle that he reiterated during the pandemic, when it was easy to become overwhelmed while working from home, balancing family, household duties, and work. He advised, "Make sure to carve out real buffer time: to catch your breath, get some exercise, or whatever you enjoy doing that helps put your mind at ease. It not only benefits you, it will benefit all of the people that count on you as well."[50]

We mentioned the use of buffer time in meetings in the first chapter of this section, though it's important to know that you can also be unapologetic about having it on your calendar, as it is just good mental-health hygiene.

There is a time limit on efficiency and productivity for any human being. In the pursuit of dogged success, there must be both a starting point and a refueling point. Always remember to find ways to reset, and be mindful of where you are on the human potential journey, keeping in mind along the way how you are influencing and being influenced by your team. Sometimes you just need a kindness break: to stop when you are in the fray and give yourself a moment to understand and appreciate your own humanity and that of others. Take a deep breath and let it out, knowing you are doing the best you can. When you (re)treat yourself with kindness and compassion, then go back to business, you will figure out solutions and have greater confidence in the direction you are taking—a direction that will lead to your continued success.

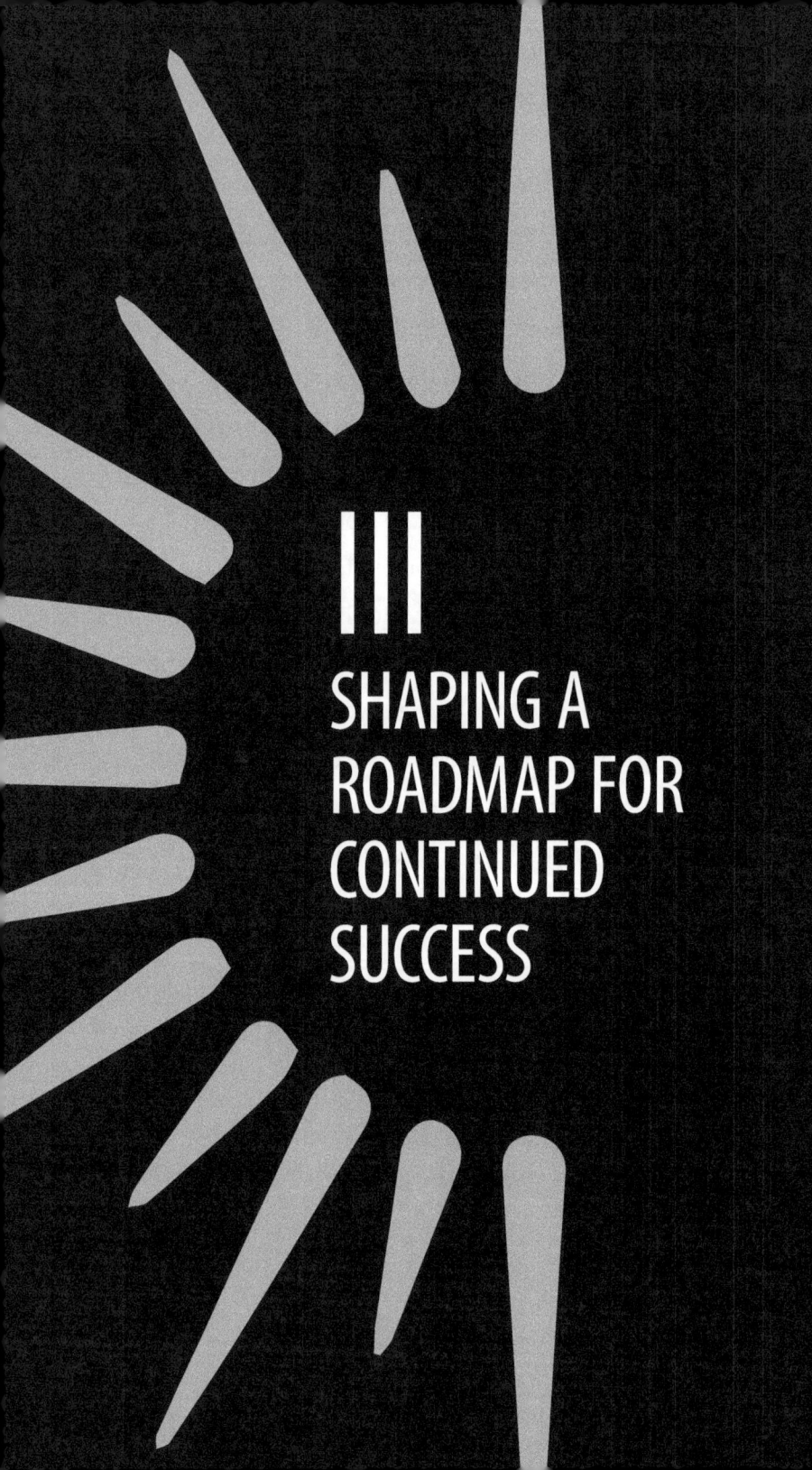

III

SHAPING A
ROADMAP FOR
CONTINUED
SUCCESS

Shaping continued success necessitates clear metrics and a steadfast dedication. Navigate business's indirect path with grace, and you will gift yourself and your organization with the realization of your truest potential.

CREATE REALISTIC LANDMARKS

Along the path to success, things aren't always going to go in a linear or upward direction.

WHERE ARE YOU on your personal growth journey? Where is your organization on its success continuum? Do you have the measures in place to ensure your progress? Will you come up short of your vision, or will your landmarks help you go the distance?

As you progress in your growth as a leader, you will be building ever-increasing self-awareness, embracing your idiosyncrasies, and infusing your uniqueness into your leadership. With charisma, authenticity, plenty of *want to*, and a clear dedication to the tasks that are yours to fulfill, you are showing up by doing your best to live the truth of free will at the highest level. Curiosity and creativity have become two of your greatest allies, allowing you to look upon the horizon and see just how great things can be and how you and your organization can capture your full creative potential. You lead with care, taking on the tough conversations with empathy and respect for others and for your mission. You are doing all of this at once, together with your team because your dogged determination is undeniable and you are dedicated to jumping in, stepping out, and empowering them. The vastness of possibility and success is exciting, though there will be real challenges, messy maneuvers, oxen in the ditches, and unexpected twists and turns to be faced. In order for everything to ultimately fall into place, there must be landmarks and specific strategies to get you there. The path to success is an indirect one, and things aren't always going to go in a linear or upward direction. In order to keep moving forward, it will become critical to have realistic landmarks to guide where you are on the authentic growth journey.

On the horizontal continuum of your desired success, two points must always be considered in parallel:

1. This is what we're facing right now.
2. This is where we want to go.

Creating realistic landmarks is like walking up a mountain. You can see the peak, but you also need to select rest spots along the way, where you will stop and reset, before setting your sights on the next landmark. Many distance runners use a technique called *fartlek* (Swedish for "speed play"), which employs this concept to improve their overall performance. As far back as eighty years ago, running coaches and scientists were experimenting with methods that could improve fitness and add variety to training. In the 1930s, Swedish Olympic athlete and coach Gösta Holmér developed fartlek training—which involves short sprints to identified landmarks, like choosing a point down the road and pushing your pace and stride to get there—as a way of combining speed and endurance. Time can then become a measurement of continued improvement. While strategic in terms of hitting a clear landmark or denoted time, fartlek training is also unstructured and leaves much of the control to the individual runner's circumstances. It is designed to allow distance runners to play around with various speeds, test their limits, and discover what ultimately works in improving their overall running endurance and speed for distance runs. The short bursts to reach identified landmarks are always part of a longer run and a bigger picture.[51]

STEP BACK (TAKE A SELAH SECOND)

So MUCH OF being a CEO is about having a "responsibility mindset"—doing what's necessary to achieve what you want Yet while you are holding yourself and others accountable, remember the power of praise and appreciation, and how the effectiveness of "job well done," said to our team or to ourselves, cannot be underestimated. Celebrate the things that have gone well and that have fostered a culture of care. Stop and take a moment to be wowed and proud of where you are in your life and in your business/career. Give yourself the perspective to see what you've already accomplished. These landmarks are as important as any other. Appreciate what you have created and contributed, and then question what else you can do! Assess what else can now be made possible by asking:

What is my next step to reach
the next landmark?

STEP INTO ACTION

BY DEFINING A clear, strategic path and landmarks to your desired success, you will help foster your personal and organizational fulfillment. Wherever the roads of leadership take you, be sure to maintain awareness of where you are at all points on the journey. Implement these strategies to help identify, create, and maximize the usefulness of strategic landmarks along the way:

1. Know Your Home Base

Every move you make and all progress you seek will begin by going within yourself. Your behavior starts with awareness of your State of Being and making sure you are in full alignment with where you want to go. Every home run you hit begins and ends with home base, which is what lies within and stems from who you are and how you are. Be in tune with that, always.

2. Know What Makes Your Team Tick

Poking around in the dark and asking your team general questions won't always lead to the truth. While I was at Tipperary, the use of Predictive Index assessments helped us understand the dynamics of the team and improved company-wide retention by 40%. Personality and behavior assessments can provide reliable tools for keeping you on track for continued success, allowing you the metrics to better know where your progress is taking you. You can use Predictive Index behavioral assessments to establish how various humans in a department could better work together, and how managers might better understand how each of their team members works best.

Looking at a personality or behavior pattern attained from an assessment and understanding what the factors represent gives you the power to have more enlightened conversations to help you get traction quickly with those you serve. You can better know who and what you are working with, what changes need to be made to reach the next landmark, and how you need to progress. What you learn from assessments becomes an asset to capitalize on, furthering and deepening your relationships, and aligning with the most important things. Use assessments as more than a hiring tool; allow them to become a coaching asset—something that further empowers you and your team to step into your fullest potential.

3. **Keep Asking Why**

   Continuing to ask *why* is key to helping you get to the root of any issue and continue to make progress. The effects of asking why are also amplified when there are two or more people doing it, challenging each other to continue to dig deeper.

It is easy to tell ourselves stories to let ourselves off the hook and veer out of alignment with the vision and precedent we set for our teams, processes, and standards—but when the walls come tumbling down or the wheels come right off the cart, it will be *on you*. That's why it's critical to set realistic landmarks in both your business progress and the path to your ultimate potential, while always maintaining awareness of yourself. Putting up a straw house will serve you fine on a sunny summer day, but when the rainstorm rolls in, you're in for it. Similarly, put up a brick house without care and insulation, and you'll likely feel the cold when the winter winds come up. Landmarks require strategic metrics. Quick fixes won't get you to your ultimate potential, and nor will most drastic actions. Each metric and landmark provides a stepping stone, further expanding your capacity for continued success.

Business will almost always take the long road. Like a slow roast, you will often need to let things simmer as you sit with them and do your absolute best to rectify or improve them, until the next thing comes along or the ideal solution is revealed. Keep rolling up your sleeves each and every day. Continue to dance between working on creating a great culture and celebrating what you have built, while keeping things in check. Staying on course will require an ongoing set of small corrections as well as big decisions when things go sideways.

But remember that when it comes to the corrections and focus required to succeed, progress doesn't just happen, it has to be intentional. You can go the distance, though you need to have patience and prioritize the people within your organization and the collective mission you are dedicating yourself to. Focus on doing what is necessary when things go wrong and taking in everything that happens as an opportunity to learn more. Open yourself to continuous growth and possibility, without the need to change things dramatically. You can remain clear and steadfast in your vision while also adapting the principles that form the foundation of your strategy to promote your own growth, that of others, and the ever-evolving nature of who you are and who your team and organization are becoming.

DEDICATE YOURSELF TO BEING A LIFELONG LEARNER

You are growing, and the growth never stops.

HOW MANY LEADERS can you help instill hope and pride in? How can you inspire others to solve things in a new way? How many people can you affect for the better, so that they then take on a transformational growth journey of their own?

While you will always need to define a clear, strategic path to your desired level of success and fulfillment, flexibility must also be built into that plan. Having that dexterity for continued growth and evolution will empower you to adapt during the times of messy maneuvers, hard conversations, and a lack of straight lines leading to solutions. This same flexibility opens the door to growth, which is the core quality of the path of a lifelong learner. What got you here won't necessarily get you "there," to that point B, C, D, E, or beyond. Work is called work for a reason, and it is filled with ebbs and flows. Growing into the ultimate leader you can become will happen only when you open yourself to learning at every turn of the evolutionary journey of leadership.

Many CEOs abide by the academic version of potential—the pragmatic steps to success that the machine grades you on: Go to college, get your MBA, grow and rise within the organization. Yet where does that leave the personal-satisfaction side of human potential—the fulfillment that stems from all that you are realizing within and for yourself, and from giving all of yourself to others? *That* is the piece our work is focused on, because now after taking the It's On You journey with us, I hope the importance of your personal satisfaction and that of your team members, through the application of your God-given ability and potential, has become clear.

Personal satisfaction ultimately comes down to continuing to learn and putting yourself in situations that allow you to do so, all while helping your team to also move into even better positions of growth and success. Ironically, "personal" satisfaction is actually less about you and more about everyone else; it is about seeing others excelling, overcoming challenges, and learning to empower themselves and others through both celebrated landmarks and tough conversations. It comes from knowing the hours, days, months, and years you have put into teaching, communicating with, giving to, and grieving with those you serve. In its truest form, personal satisfaction is composed of your happiness, fulfillment, prosperity, and contentment. It is the acceptance that you are growing and the knowledge that change and growth *never stop*. It touches all levels of our being—the mental, emotional, spiritual, financial, and physical—as well as the ultimate acceptance that you are:

- Unique

- Different

- Evolving

- Able to influence in the best way possible

STEP BACK (TAKE A SELAH SECOND)

WHETHER YOU'RE ACHIEVING a grand success or finding yourself face-to-face with a daunting challenge, consider these two questions we use in my Vistage peer group, which can inspire great learning:

- *What's working well?*

- *What would be even better if ... ?*

Sit with these questions when you feel you have hit a bump in the road or rescued the ox from the ditch. Look at the victories first, and then look at what you perceive as failures. As you gain awareness and become more self-actualized, my hope is that you will step further into seeing your victories and failures as equal. Success is all in how you look the bumps and how you use all the information to keep going and keep growing. It may work out, or it may not. The good news is that if it doesn't, you get to use your free will to find the next thing that *will* work.

STEP INTO ACTION

WHEREVER THE ROADS of leadership take you, it's critical to maintain awareness of who you are and where you are at all points on the journey. Here are some strategies you can implement to become a true lifelong learner and leader:

1. **Remain True to You**

   A big part of the growth journey means wholly recognizing what you will bring to the role that will be beneficial to others and to you. Be real about what is true for you, about what is going right at this moment (and what is not), and about where you want to go. Stay open to growing and sharpening your leadership on an ongoing basis, and never veer away from the strategies in this book, because when you do, you may lose your connection to the best parts of yourself.

2. **Try Things On**

   As you forge your path on the evolutionary journey to leadership, you will inevitably question yourself at times. Sometimes finding your way takes trial and error. It is okay to try things on, see how they fit, and run with them for a bit. In those trial periods, you will intuit the things that are a good fit for you—the things that are part of your calling—and those that are not. Like changing gears on a bicycle, once you find the right mode, you'll quickly hit your stride.

3. Have Something to Fall Back On

Not every idea is great. Not every idea is going to work. But every idea that comes into your mind is valid. There's a reason that idea came into your mind in the first place. CEOs often have this "other notebook" where we write down the things we *think* we know and the things we *think* will work. Make notes about every learning experience you have. Revisit those notes and make them your script and your muse. Reviewing them will prompt you to remember the emotional imprint that a certain situation or interaction had on you. When I was learning from Byron (and going through graduate school in a new state), he imprinted himself on me in a big way. It was important for me to create a guide and outlet for myself through notes. My notebook eventually became that something I could fall back on as I encountered all the new experiences and situations I faced as CEO. As you are simultaneously doing your daily work, meeting with the board, and meeting with your team, you then have this collection of thoughts captured, which you can keep revisiting in your mind.

4. Review the Big Decisions

Messes are going to happen, and there is no shame in redirection. Some messes, you will need to ride out and learn from; with others, you will need to know when to alter your course. The metric may be off or the goal may be inaccurate. A smart next step is always analysis. To unpack what occurred and figure out why it didn't work, you can do an After Action Review (AAR), just as Jocko Willink and his Navy SEAL team did following their Iraq mission. AARs were formally developed as a debriefing tool by the US Army. The Center for Evidence-Based

Management defines an AAR as the process of reflecting on a project during and after its completion in order to assess your performance and identify and learn from successes and failures. The structured review or debriefing process is designed to engage an open and honest professional dialogue. It is based on four key questions:

- *What was expected to happen?*

- *What actually occurred?*

- *What went well, and why?*

- *What can be improved, and how?* [52]

Realistically, you will both remember and interpret your failures more than your victories. When you are truly living in your authentic self, however, you aren't judging things as "good" and "bad," because when the unexpected happens, you know that it provides a chance to look at things differently, through the lens of opportunity. Learning from victories as well as losses requires awareness and humility. It may be tempting to beat yourself up when you try something and it doesn't work, but it would be far worse not to give something a shot. The fear of failure gets perfectionists in trouble, because nothing is perfect, and some things are bound to fail. You also won't always know the difference between something that truly isn't right and something that is simply a bump in an otherwise right path. Losses or missed results are really just a license to go out and crush it all over again.

Being a lifelong learner requires living in a state of wonder, with a deep appreciation for the awe-inspiring nature of life, human interaction, and all that we are capable of together. It necessitates a willingness to improve after failures and to make the time to celebrate accomplishments. As you progress in your leadership, take everything as an opportunity for growth. Continue to ask yourself what you really need—to be doing or not doing, to have or not have—and who you want to become. Open yourself to an ongoing dialogue with others about yourself. Push yourself to learn new things daily, because opportunities for discovery exist everywhere.

When you choose to talk yourself beyond your comfort zone, rather than off the ledge, that is where the invisible bridge shows up that takes you to the next peak ... the one that leads you even closer to all that you want to be, do, and have. All of this can be made easier when you open yourself to being a curious lifelong learner and take the time to build a support system. Becoming and being CEO can take you on a lonely route fraught with challenges and moments of second-guessing. That is why having a coach or mentor is critical. They will be your guide and springboard to help ensure forward momentum. I didn't become CEO doing it on my own, and nor can you. No one travels this journey alone, and self-actualization doesn't happen in a bubble. That said, you are ultimately the one who needs to lead, taking ownership and accountability and doing the work, because the learning, teaching, growth, evolving, and empowerment *is on you*. There is a vastness to your potential as a leader and as a human being, and it is up to you how far into it you are willing to venture.

What will your next step be? Maybe it is to reach a point where you graduate and move on to another opportunity that allows you to better grow in alignment with what you stand for. Maybe you want to build your organization to the point of being able to turn a great company over to another great CEO, who then gets their opportunity to lead. You can go on to board work, community work, or volunteer work, while you pass along the treasures you have learned to new leaders and to all those they serve. The journey never ends, as you will always go on to serve in other capacities. What matters is who you are and how you are bring that to the table, applying confidence to your problem-solving, status-quo–shifting, corporation-building, and challenge-defying abilities.

You pave the way to your own ultimate potential, and it's on you to decide just how great that potential is. Let this vision move you to the heights of your success and to find the best in yourself, and so empowering others to reach theirs. And may *It's On You* be your compass on this continuously evolving path.

ABOUT THE AUTHOR

MARTHA PERCIVAL BROWN is the former chief executive officer of Tipperary Sales, Inc. (La-Z-Boy Southeast). A proven retail industry executive and franchise expert, she has transformed companies, cultures, and leaders. As the first woman to lead her multigenerational, family-owned retail furniture company, Martha

 has secured the status of Tipperary Sales, Inc., as one of the most successful retail furniture companies in the US, having grown the organization to a team of 170 employees, exceeding revenue over $70 million. *Furniture Today*, the

industry's premier publication, named the company one of the top 100 stores in America multiple years over.

Martha is a visionary leader who knows what it takes to strengthen and evolve a company's competitiveness and leadership in an ever-changing world. At the forefront of her work lies an exceptional passion for the development of people. Throughout her multi-decade career, she has shaped her company's culture to attract, develop, and retain key talent. She established the company's first formal community relations program, transformed her company's learning and development function into "Tipperary University," and established The Tipperary Way, which outlines the critical fundamentals that strategically align hundreds of employees across all store locations throughout the Southeast. She has also served on the executive committee for the board of trustees of Columbia College, SC, where she earned her bachelor's degree in English and communication, as well as on the board of directors for Ronald McDonald House, Charlotte. She also holds an EMBA from the McColl School of Business at Queens University of Charlotte.

After retiring as CEO in December 2023, Martha transitioned into the role of board member and coach to aspiring CEOs and leaders. The lessons in this book are those she has lived and now chooses to teach. They are the product of bumps, bruises, and moments of intuition and insight that worked out for the best, designed to help others find their groove and rise to their potential.

ENDNOTES

1   "Leadership Initiatives," Queens University of Charlotte, McColl School of Business, https://www.queens.edu/academics/schools-colleges/mccoll-school/about-us/leadership-initiatives.html.

2   Jocko Willink, "Extreme Ownership," TEDxUniversity ofNevada, February 2, 2017, https://www.youtube.com/watch?v=ljqra3BcqWM.

3   Arthur Rubens, Gerald A. Schoenfeld, Bryan S. Schaffer, and Joseph S. Leah; "Self-awareness and leadership: Developing an individual strategic professional development plan in an MBA leadership course"; Science Direct, March 2018, https://www.sciencedirect.com/science/article/abs/pii/S1472811716301732.

4   Patrick Lencioni, "Are you an ideal team player?", TEDxUniversityofNevada, February, 2020, https://www.ted.com/talks/patrick_lencioni_are_you_an_ideal_team_player.

5   Adi Ignatius and Hubert Joly, "Former Best Buy CEO Hubert Joly: Empowering Workers to Create 'Magic'," Harvard Business

Review, Dec 2, 2021, https://hbr.org/2021/12/former-best-bu
y-ceo-hubert-joly-empowering-workers-to-create-magic.

6   Hubert Joly, "A New Leadership Model for the Future of
    Business and Work," Harvard Business Review, June 14, 2021,
    https://hbr.org/webinar/2021/06/a-new-leadership-model-for
    -the-future-of-business-and-work.

7   Ignatius and Joly, "Former Best Buy CEO Hubert Joly."

8   Ignatius and Joly, "Former Best Buy CEO Hubert Joly."

9   Anne Trafton, "In the Blink of an Eye," MIT News, January 16,
    2014, https://news.mit.edu/2014/in-the-blink-of-an-eye-0116.

10 The Napa Wine Project, "Dark Matter Wines," https://www.
    napawineproject.com/dark-matter-wines/.

11 Dark Matter Wines, "Mondavi Sisters," https://www.dark-
    matterwines.com/about-us.

12 Roy F. Baumeister, "Free Will in Scientific Psychology",
    Perspectives on Psychological Science, January 1, 2008, https://
    journals.sagepub.com/doi/10.1111/j.1745-6916.2008.00057.x.

13 Chip Cutter, "Warren Buffett Says Bad Leaders Pose Biggest
    Risk to Companies," The Wall Street Journal, May 3, 2021,
    https://www.wsj.com/articles/warren-buffett-says-bad-leader
    s-pose-biggest-risk-to-companies-11620034201.

14 Bill George, Authentic Leadership (Hoboken: Jossey-Bass, 2004)

15 Rob Goffee and Gareth Jones, "Managing Authenticity:
    The Paradox of Great Leadership," Harvard Business
    Review, December 2005, https://hbr.org/2005/12/managin
    g-authenticity-the-paradox-of-great-leadership.

16 Allison Morrow, "Citigroup's Jane Fraser is doing the un-thinkable on Wall Street," CNN Business, November 15, 2021, https://edition.cnn.com/2021/11/15/business/jane-fraser-citigroup-risk-takers/index.html.

17 Allison Morrow, "Citigroup's Jane Fraser is doing the un-thinkable on Wall Street."

18 Nick DeLissio, "The Restoration of the Acropolis," Penn State Archaeological Preservation blog, February 20, 2014, https://sites.psu.edu/archeologicalpreservation/2014/02/20/the-restoration-of-the-acropolis/.

19 Allison Morrow, "Wall Street's biggest WFH advocate is bringing underperforming staff back into the office," CNN Business, January 18, 2023, https://www.cnn.com/2023/01/18/business/citi-work-from-home-jane-fraser/index.html.

20 "Brené Brown Reveals Which Four Skill Sets Make the Best Leaders," The Tonight Show with Jimmy Fallon, November 11, 2020, https://www.youtube.com/watch?v=HqetWsb28Mo.

21 Julie Riddle, "Attitude Matters," Whitworth Today Magazine, Fall 2018, https://www.whitworth.edu/cms/our-stories/magazine/colin-powell/.

22 Julie Riddle, "Attitude Matters"

23 Jim Collins, Good to Great (New York: Random House Business, 2001). Quoted at https://www.jimcollins.com/concepts/first-who-then-what.html

24 Jay Acunzo, "When You Need to Be Creative, Constraints Are Your Strengths [The Story of Unsplash]," Marketing Show

Runners, June 12, 2018, https://www.marketingshowrunners.com/blog/unsplash-constraints/.

25 "The History of Unsplash," Unsplash.com, https://unsplash.com/history.

26 Gita Johar, "Creativity is in the Eye of the Beholder," Columbia University, March 23, 2016, https://www8.gsb.columbia.edu/video/videos/gita-johar-creativity-eye-beholder.

27 Shayna Joubert, "The Importance of Creativity in Business," Northeastern University Graduate Programs blog, November 9, 2017, https://www.northeastern.edu/graduate/blog/creativity-importance-in-business/.

28 The Order of Saint Helena, https://www.osh.org/.

29 Marianne Williamson, A Return to Love (San Francisco: HarperOne, 1996).

30 Emilie Griffin, The Reflective Executive (Eugene, Oregon: Wipf and Stock, 2008).

31 Steven Conmy, "What does culture eats strategy for breakfast mean?" Corporate Governance Institute, May 4, 2022, https://www.thecorporategovernanceinstitute.com/insights/lexicon/what-does-culture-eats-strategy-for-breakfast-mean/.

32 Susan Scott, "Why Fierce," Executive Speakers Bureau https://www.youtube.com/watch?v=gYR6QBitTsg.

33 Emily Farra, "Patagonia Has a New Mission to 'Save Our Home Planet'—One of Its First Employees Explains How They'll Get It Done," Vogue, November 9, 2021, https://www.

vogue.com/article/patagonia-cfda-award-climate-chang
e-ambitions-vincent-stanley.

34 Patagonia.com, "1% for the Planet," https://www.patagonia.
com/one-percent-for-the-planet.html.

35 Patagonia.com, "Activism," https://www.patagonia.com/
activism/.

36 Jeff Beer, "Exclusive: "Patagonia is in business to save our
home planet," Fast Company, December 13, 2018, https://
www.fastcompany.com/90280950/exclusive-patagonia-is-i
n-business-to-save-our-home-planet.

37 Patagonia.com, "Our Core Values," https://www.patagonia.
com/core-values/.

38 Emily Farra, "Patagonia Has a New Mission to 'Save Our
Home Planet.'"

39 Cheryl A. Bachelder, "The CEO of Popeyes on Treating
Franchisees as the Most Important Customers," Harvard
Business Review, October 2016, https://hbr.org/2016/10/th
e-ceo-of-popeyes-on-treating-franchisees-as-the-most-imp
ortant-customers.

40 Cheryl A. Bachelder, "The CEO of Popeyes on Treating
Franchisees as the Most Important Customers"

41 Allan Lee, Sara Willis, and Amy Wei Tian; "When Empowering
Employees Works, and When It Doesn't," Harvard Business
Review, March 2, 2018, https://hbr.org/2018/03/whe
n-empowering-employees-works-and-when-it-doesnt.

42 Elisabet Lahti, "Sisu: Answering the Call of Adventure with Strength and Grace," in Paula Reid & Eric Brymer (eds.), Adventure Psychology: Going Knowingly into the Unknown (New York: Routledge, 2022).

43 R.P. Hämäläinen and E. Saarinen, "Systems Intelligent Leadership," in R. P. Hämäläinen & E. Saarinen (eds.), Systems Intelligence in Leadership and Everyday Life (Helsinki: Systems Analysis Laboratory, Helsinki University of Technology, 2007).

44 C.D. Broad, Scientific Thought (San Diego: Harcourt, Brace, and Company, 1923), p. 68.

45 "Fire Lookouts", Forest History Society https://foresthistory.org/research-explore/us-forest-service-history/policy-and-law/fire-u-s-forest-service/fire-lookouts/.

46 Lauren Eskreis-Winkler, James J. Gross, and Angela L. Duckworth; "Grit: Sustained Self-Regulation in the Service of Superordinate Goals".

47 Eskreis-Winkler, Gross, Duckworth, "Grit."

48 Brené Brown, "Dare to Lead | True belonging never asks us to change who we are," brenebrown.com, https://brenebrown.com/art/true-belonging/.

49 Natalie Rice, Mary Stevens, and Nate Skid; "Why LinkedIn CEO Jeff Weiner leaves 90 minutes of his schedule empty every day," CNBC, August 23, 2018; https://www.cnbc.com/video/2018/08/23/why-linkedin-ceo-jeff-weiner-leaves-90-minutes-of-his-schedule-empty-every-day.html

50 Jeff Weiner, LinkedIn, 2020, https://www.linkedin.com/posts/jeffweiner08_for-those-fortunate-enough-to-have-the-opportunity-activity-6659505767818805248-k210.

51 Tom Craggs, "What is a fartlek run and how can it help you get faster?" Runners World, July 24, 2023, https://www.runnersworld.com/uk/training/a36362823/fartlek-run/.

52 "Guide to the After Action Review," Version 1.1, Center for Evidence-Based Management, October 2010, https://www.ecdc.europa.eu/sites/default/files/documents/Protocol-for-focused-AAR-on-evidence-based-decision-making-COVID-19.pdf.